18-1

BADGERS
on the Highland Edge

BADGERS

on the Highland Edge

JIM CRUMLEY

JONATHAN CAPE
LONDON

First published 1994

1 3 5 7 9 10 8 6 4 2

© Jim Crumley 1994

Jim Crumley has asserted his right
under the Copyright, Designs and Patents Act, 1988
to be identified as the author of this work

First published in the United Kingdom in 1994 by
Jonathan Cape
Random House, 20 Vauxhall Bridge Road, London SW1V 2SA

Random House Australia (Pty) Limited
20 Alfred Street, Milsons Point, Sydney,
New South Wales 2061, Australia

Random House New Zealand Limited
18 Poland Road, Glenfield,
Auckland 10, New Zealand

Random House South Africa (Pty) Limited
PO Box 337, Bergvlei, South Africa

Random House UK Limited Reg. No. 954009

A CIP catalogue record for this book
is available from the British Library

ISBN 0–224–03642–4

Typeset by Deltatype Ltd, Ellesmere Port, Cheshire
Printed in Great Britain by
Mackays of Chatham plc, Chatham, Kent

Contents

Illustrations

For Keith Graham

Acknowledgements

The sum of badger literature is distinguished by nothing more telling than Ernest Neal's *The Natural History of Badgers* (Christopher Helm, 1986). It is all that a definitive monograph should be, and a marvel of clarity and modest expertise to a novice like me. In a very different vein (but doubtless the two would have had the highest regard for each other) the late David Stephen was a great badger champion both in literature and in the field. His *Bodach the Badger* (Century, 1983) and *Highland Animals* (Highlands and Islands Development Board, 1974) are the fiction and the non-fiction of him, and masterly both. These were all the writings I referred to, and given the nature of this book, all I needed.

Thanks, too, to Brian Cadzow for sowing the seeds of the whole idea, to the Craig family who inhabit the Highland Edge, to Mike Harris of the Grampian Badger Survey and Don MacCaskill for photographs, and to Keith Graham, who is everywhere in these pages.

Finally my thanks to Ratty and Mole and Kenneth Grahame. *The Wind in the Willows* has been a part of my life for a long time. I have a greater appreciation now than ever before of how good a book it is.

Spell for Safe Badgers

Roof well timbered with
root of limber living tree.
Giving of courage. Stealth.

Thatch of bracken. Health of cubs.
Wealth of scratch places to lay bare.
Home patch lardered with worms. Peace.
Fleece of stars.

Wind far-carrying. Cool marrying
of water and dark earth.
Dearth of gun, gas, dog, trap, poison,
noisome men and all their sour scents.

Otherwise
just leave us
alone.

Jim Crumley
Summer, 1993

I

The Bliss of Ignorance

The mole had long wanted to make the acquaintance of the
Badger. He seemed, by all accounts, to be such an important per-
sonage and, though rarely visible, to make his unseen influence
felt by everybody about the place... 'It's all right,' the Rat would
say. 'Badger'll turn up some day or other – he's always turning
up ... but you must not only take him *as* you find him, but *when*
you find him.'

– Kenneth Grahame
The Wind in the Willows

H E FLOATED FACE-DOWN in a derelict mill pond and I lifted him by
the scruff of his broken neck. I suppose it was thirty years ago. I
was a teenager with a bike and the wild world was a barely prised oyster
crammed with pearls, but what I lifted from the water was not one of
them. He was a huge old badger boar, shapeless as a bad cushion, for he
had been smashed and wounded many times. Perhaps he had been taken
alive by what keepers at the sharp edge of nature call 'the terrier boys', to
be sold on to 'the pit bull boys', although it is said they get more money
for an old sow. She puts up more of a fight, a better show. Then, as
now, contempt is reason enough for the death of a badger.

Across his sodden fur writhed a white horde of maggots. I dropped
the mass where I had found it and was at once helplessly sick. After
several minutes bent double in the bracken, I straightened to find the
black and unblinking eye of a robin watching me, side-headed, from an
old fencepost a yard away. He flew down on to the floating corpse,
plundered a deft beakful of maggots, and perched again on the post just
long enough for me to establish that the maggots still writhed. By the

time he was cramming them into the small yellow yawns of a clutch of nestlings in a bramble bush I was being sick again.

It was a bizarre introduction to badgers. Curiously, for years afterwards it put me off badgers rather than robins. It also established all too indelibly an association which puzzles me still: where there are badgers there are robins.

So that was the first badger I ever saw. The second, third and fourth were glimpsed crossing a motorway during the pre-dawn winter darkness of sluggish early morning commuter journeys to an Edinburgh newspaper office, dark and curious blurs on my loathed daily ritual. It seems strange to me now that I never once paused long enough to note the position of what was probably a regular badger route, but 7 a.m. was never my best time of day. Perhaps it was just the conspiracy at work.

The conspiracy worked in mysterious ways. It began in earnest while I was researching my book *Waters of the Wild Swan*. Brian Cadzow, a retired Lothian farmer who had greatly assisted that venture, asked an unexpected question:

'Have you ever written about badgers? You should. Super creatures.'

I responded without enthusiasm.

'Well, let me know if you ever want to watch badgers. I'll show you a couple of places.' He reiterated the offer so often over the next year or so in the face of my polite indifference that eventually a seed of a kind was sown, though hardly one that I nurtured.

Then, with the swan book finished and time hanging heavy, I drifted idly to a pond where I had spent many swan-watching hours. I kicked my heels moodily through one afernoon, trying to set up swan photographs in the warm, flat afternoon light. It had been in my mind to drop in on the Cadzows who live beside the pond, and I was disappointed to find no-one in. I sat on, thinking about the hours I had spent with the swans here, hours scattered over years, and many more hours scattered over many other landscapes. At once, and with no blinding flash of inspiration, I thought I would like to attempt the opposite kind of book, one which would not fall back on years of research but would be a quest, discovering as it went along. Then, because Brian Cadzow was also on my mind, the conspiracy suddenly clicked a one-word possibility into place: badgers. I had never watched badgers, and all I knew of them was the little I had stumbled across in pursuit of something else. By three in the morning I was halfway through *Bodach the Badger*, David Stephen's novel about Highland badgers which had been pressed on me a year before by moutaineer Hamish Brown ... the conspiracy again.

Now I was intrigued. Could I go out among badgers and write about them on their terms and mine? I knew precious little of what their terms might be. My own would use that quality of ignorance which is blissfully blessed by an absence of preconception. Simplicity would be everything. I would work with what I could carry in a small rucksack. I would photograph with what I could hold in my hands, and invested in a sophisticated flash-biased camera which claimed to render even that fraught realm of dusk or darkness photography simple. Simple. I wrote the word down so often, simple, simple, simple, that I stopped recognising the shape of the word on the page, and I tried to snuff out the warning voice in my ear which counselled that nothing in nature was *that* simple. But I was excited at the prospect of giving the purist in me its head without even knowing if I would *like* badgers.

I told myself to trust instinct. Seek to make sense and sensibility among strangers, and if by the end of it all I reduced the distance between badgers and me, I would have a book. If I had nothing to show for it all, I would turn my back on badgers and go back to the bright mountain world above ground and under the sky where I am at home.

I went back to see Brian Cadzow, and for a good hour, well fuelled by vat-sized whiskies, we talked badgers and setts and what to do and what not to do. Due to a temporary state of immobility while he awaited a new hip, he recruited a friend to point me in the right direction. Suddenly I had four setts at my disposal without breaking sweat.

The first sett looked unpromising, a few yards from a public foot-path. The badgers may be able to live with such disturbance, but not me. If I was going to be sitting alone in a wood intent on meeting badgers head-on, I wanted to be alone in it, not exchanging pleasantries with dog walkers, horse-riders, mountain bikers, poachers and court-ing couples as we used to say. The second sett was huge and would be worthy of a lifetime's study on its own, but it was in the grounds of a large working building – too much light and noise, too many people to see me coming and going, and to ask questions. Brian said the sett would be recognisable by a small white hunt gate at the top of the bank. I found the sett but not the gate, at least not at first. When I did finally fall over it, it was decrepit and slowly being reclaimed by nature as a rotting timbery mulch. There was no visible vestige of white paint. I asked Brian when he had last seen the gate.

'Oh, a few years ago now.'

'There isn't a scrap of white paint on it, you know.'

'Really? Well, there was when I put it in fifty years ago.'

The third sett was in a small circular wood which stood like a coronet among high fields, but there was only one small entrance. The spoil heap by the hole was black with coal. True to their West Lothian origins, these badgers were miners. I viewed the place as a dismal prospect.

The fourth sett was in a dark wood alongside a farm road. There were thirty holes, it was obviously busy, and there was even a bank within the wood upon which I could sit in some comfort (a relative term in a wood at night) without worrying about my scent reaching the badgers as they emerged from the main entrances twenty feet away and several feet below me. This, it would appear from advice which had begun to rain down on me from seasoned badger-watchers, was the first commandment. Get high, preferably up a tree, and then you will only have to worry about not being seen or heard, so be still and silent as well. There was a second commandment, a kind of adjunct to the first, which I have encountered in a dozen different sources – get there an hour before sunset. Months later, watching a boar badger leave his sett under a mountain five minutes after I had examined his sett in great detail, I learned a new first commandment – get lucky.

My one reservation about this seemingly ideal West Lothian sett was that even in summer sunlight it was a bit dark. I dislike dark woods at night.

Then, at a discreet cough from the conspiracy, I began to be troubled by the fact that the sett had been handed to me on a plate with no effort on my part. The purist in me has always held the joy of discovery as the highest prize – the only truly worthwhile prize – of watching nature. Here I was denied it. I also had the first inkling of the elusive nature of the perspective I sought.

The conspiracy knew what it was doing. It reasoned that my own instinctive perseverance and patience in the face of nature's adversity (I take no credit for it, but I give thanks for it often) would whittle away the difficulties until a gleaming solution presented itself. The conspiracy was right, but then conspiracies of nature usually are. They can also be ponderous, painstaking, and not a little perverse. That perversity dogged me through what was left of summer, the whole of the autumn and a quite thankless winter, when badger-watching is a notoriously fickle art. There were consoling hints of badgers, clues to their passage, glimpses even, but as a quarry they simply grew more elusive as my luck grew more wretched and my ignorance only deepened.

But through it all I carried a small flame, David Stephen's word-perfect portrait of what it was I was looking for:

> The badger is bear-like, squat, big-clawed, hand-footed, hen-toed and out at elbow, with the bear's inswinging shambling gait. He is giant of frame, heavy of bone, broad of chest, sheathed in muscle, strong-jawed, powerful, retiring, tolerant, non-aggressive, and a terrible fighting machine, but he is the last only when self-effacement, turning the other cheek and the peace conference have failed. Once he goes to war, he can break a terrier's jaw, cripple a collie, kill a fox, or take the hand off a man.

It was, I thought, as well to know.

2

Winter of Discontent

Y OU ENTER THE WOOD by the broken sink. The track you follow is of the badgers' making. The sink sits there like a turnstile. You half expect it to say 'Way In', but all it says is 'Shanks'. Whoever dumped it, however long ago (long enough for it to look rooted and wear an encroachment of moss), would not know that in torchlight from twenty yards away it will lead you, sure as lighthouses, from the main sett to the edge of the wood in the pitchest black of midnights. Bear left at the holly tree and head for the sink.

To me, it is landmark and irritant. It shouldn't be there. But I use it. To the badgers, it is part of the furniture of the wood, like nettles, but not as useful. Nearby is a toy car, a plastic Porsche in racing trim, also dumped. I have watched a robin stand on its roof, a pause between the two legs of a flight from ash to sycamore. Does the bird notice? Does it like the colours? There is a splash of bird droppings on the bonnet, corrupting the colour scheme, also the work of the robin, and a fitting comment by nature on those who dump things in woods, down banks, over cliffs, in quarries, that contemptuous out-of-sight-ness which amounts to out-of-mind only for whoever dumped it. In the wood, it's only a sink, and a toy car, and clearly the wildlife is unperturbed, but I feel as if the wood has been violated. It is not even much of a wood, little more than a wide shelter belt two hundred yards by a hundred, a loose plantation of larch and spruce with wide fringes of ash and sycamore, holly and nettles, bits of birch and bracken and bramble. The badgers have been here for fifty years at least, possibly much more, long enough to redesign the woodland floor massively, reshaping its contours with prodigious earthworks. The two biggest spoil heaps at the two biggest entrances to the sett are twenty feet wide and four feet high. Each day, or almost each day, they grow a little more. But it is the badger's privilege to tamper with the woodland, for he is nature reshaping and reworking nature.

I first walked the wood in summer sunlight, in late August, a warm and dappled place, but dappled darkly, something I should have been more wary of at once, but I missed the hidden tension of the dark shades. I set about learning for myself where the badgers lived and the company they kept there, the sights and sounds and scents of their woodland kin. Walking the wood from front to back, I should have paid more attention to the sense of mild relief in stepping from the darkest trees to the boundary dyke and the open field and sky beyond, but I didn't.

I sat in a small pool of sunlight with my back to a middle-aged sycamore on the top of the woodland bank above the main sett. The plantation trees creep almost to the top of the bank from behind, a curtain eighty yards deep which would always shield me from the worst of the prevailing weather and snuff out the wind. Any skinny snakes of wind which did find their way through would carry my scent clear over the badgers' heads until they became so accustomed to me that they would treat me with the same indifference they accorded the sink, or I became as rooted to their woodland as the sycamore where I sat. I was comfortable and confident and, it seemed on that warm afternoon, I had achieved the perfect badger-watching niche at the first attempt. All I had to do now was to turn up two or three times a week for as long as it took, sit still, watch and write down what I saw. I could have done it that way, too, but the most devious twists of the conspiracy still lay before me out of sight, hidden round an unturned corner of the year.

I examined the spoil heaps, the great mounds by the age-old entrances worn smooth by uncounted badger generations, the new additions further out in the wood where the spoil was too loose and flimsy to stub a toe. Something glittered in the sunlight on the top of the biggest spoil heap. Glass. More bloody litter, I snarled. Then I found more glass, and more, bottles, old bottles, mostly intact, and pieces of china. I spent a painstaking hour clearing glass away from the setts, convinced the badgers, especially cubs if they were around, could be injured by the broken pieces. I told myself I was performing a service, and would have to go on performing it. The badgers, in their compulsive daily diggings, were obviously unearthing an old midden from a long demolished farmhouse. Days later, flicking through Ernest Neal's famed monograph *The Natural History of Badgers*, I chanced on a paragraph entitled 'Miscellaneous Items' in a chapter about diet. 'Badgers do not confine themselves to the edible,' it began, followed by an account of badgers crunching glass with their teeth and spitting out the pieces. I stopped tidying up spoil heaps after that.

More than an hour before sunset I was back at the sycamore, but now it was unlit and the sun no longer dappled the wood. Strange, I thought, so little light on such a beautiful evening.

I have always loved the end of the day, the dusk sloping down into the dark, that knife-edge of nature when the daylight creatures withdraw and the night ones emerge, and briefly the two most fundamental elements of nature overlap. It seems to me the most natural thing in the world to stay out late, dallying with nature. Dawns I was never so good at, unless I had dallied all night. Here I sat, working with the grain of nature, and although I was in an unfamiliar wood far from my mountain element and felt a glimmer of unease in my surroundings, I was well set up for the task in hand, and waiting. Four hours later, stiff and sore and badger-less, I rose, walked to the car and drove gloomily the thirty motorway miles home, wondering what I had done wrong.

Mid-September, an hour-and-a-half before sunset with three more blank nights behind me and three mornings-after which declared in the earth and the spoil heaps and the dung pits (with which badgers pock-mark the fringes of a busy sett) that there had been badgers about, that I had left too early, or perhaps that I was not still enough or discreet enough or high enough or quiet enough, at ease enough, or just not seeing enough. I would persevere. Badgers, according to Dr Neal, will accustom themselves to almost anything in time. Here they were already inured to the passage of farm traffic noise and headlights no more than two yards from the main sett. There was no reason to assume they would not in time accustom themselves to me. So I sat, and as the day ebbed and the dusk flowed I let my eyes wander and widen and worked with my ears.

The evening rush hour in the neighbourhood rookery put a monstrous regiment five hundred strong on the air, all laughing like Satchmo, and when its gravelly discordance finally subsided, the quiet which followed at once was the profoundest thing in the landscape of the dusk.

The only bird still singing in the wood was a robin. Robinsong in September is a flutey, lyrical thing which holds none of the aggressive fortissimos of the nesting season. It is tempting to think of it as the song for the sake of the song, that it's something from which the bird actually derives pleasure. A soft answering chorus from a far corner of the wood suggested that it also holds at least an element of territorial assertion.

Stillness and silence reward any nature-watcher. The nearer robin perched four feet away and began again to sing. I saw the beak open and the throat working and heard the pure silver stream of sound emerge and hang on its small piece of air. The song stopped and the robin threw me a vivid side-headed reminder of that thirty-year-old dead badger day, then flew down to the largest of the sett's spoil heaps and began to forage there, stabbing often at the freshly excavated earth. Perhaps that is part of the attraction of badger setts for robins, the mites and ticks and fleas which inhabit a badger's coat are scratched and groomed out and dumped by their host on his doorstep. A robin can dine richly there. He paused again to sing, so close to the largest sett entrance that the song must have echoed and rushed down its passages and through its chambers like a mountain burn in spate. How familiar the badgers' darkened days must be with near or distant echoes of that sound.

A squabble of jackdaws fell on the wood, monkey-chattering, cutting short the robin which now stood tall (that is, about four inches), listening. The chattering receded, the robin relaxed and flew a few yards to another scrap of the wood's human litter. What looked like a photographer's printing tray, a curious cast-off, lay by a secondary badger hole. As it always held rain water for as long as I came to know it, it was a perfect drinking vessel for robins. So my robin drank. A robin drinking is microscopic theatre. The whole body tips up and reaches down. A beakful is never going to cause tidal waves, but only the tip dips in, and so briefly that it seems inconceivable that any amount of water at all has been taken. Then the body tips back to its tallest pose, the head tips further back and the drink is drunk, relished, and the body tips stiffly down for the next sip, scarcely troubling the surface. It is as though he doesn't so much drink as pick drops from the water's skin in the way he picks maggots from a dead badger or fleas from the badger's doormat. If it was music, it would be a triangle struck with a feather. So he drank, and having drunk, he jumped in. The bath was everything in water the drinking was not, so that you are amazed there is so much water in an inch. It lasted five frantic minutes, then the bird flew off into the gloom and I heard no more of him that night.

Not so the blackbirds. They had assembled in the smaller wood on the other side of the farm road, a hellish black legion sallying on the warpath. In a wood like this one, the sound of a squad of stone masons berserkly hewing granite is usually a hit squad of blackbirds abusing a tawny owl. The owl would be standing sentry stiff, back to a trunk, feet splayed across the girth of a fat limb, trying to persuade the rest of the wild wood that here was no owl but a piece of woody pine with ears and swivelling eyes. Blackbirds are rarely fooled by this. The owl knows they know, and sooner or later it will weary of their sustained abuse and fly to another trunk. There it will pretend to be a piece of woody ash, and that won't fool the blackbirds either. The mob will pursue and reconvene, and so the ritual goes on until either the owl vacates the wood or the dusk grows too dark for the blackbirds. At this time of day, the dusk darkened beyond the pale and the blackbirds called a halt.

A new voice: a bellicose thing, guttural too, with a hint of swagger, a clatter in the branches behind me, punctuated by short, quiet croaks, the vocabulary of magpies. Somewhere away to my left was a wren going on and on and on, the way wrens do, and following dowdily in the robin's tracks by the sett, a dunnock crept. The wood darkened, and having darkened, blackened. I sat without a torch, and while a whiff of ground mist moved in among the fields beyond the wood, a swithering unease touched me from behind. I tried to identify it, but it flittered, bat-like, just beyond my mind's reach. The badgers should be emerging soon, I told myself, and convinced that I had excelled myself at stillness and silence, I was sure they would. I was never to be so sure again.

I heard them before I saw them for, however they emerged, it was not by the huge main entrance I was watching. What I heard was a heavy-footed rustling on the woodland floor, beyond the one sett entrance which faced away from me. I stared at the sound through perhaps twenty yards of pitch dark. It was like looking for an idea in a fog. Shapes moved, or did they? David Stephen had pronounced that the white on the badger's face was a shade 'no darkness could conceal'. So why was it concealed by this one?

Why the hell did I forgo the torch?

What's so special about my eyes?

Whatever made me think I could do this?

Doubt had me, and was making mincemeat of my thought processes when a pale blur moved and hardened into a kind of pied and mobile jigsaw puzzle with pieces missing. The jigsaw consolidated in turn into the white face of a badger minus the two black stripes which curve over the ears and hide the eyes and almost touch its nose. In that woodland blackness, only the white of the face showed, and the grey-black bulk of a barely definable shadow followed it.

Other faces now sharpened into focus, and moved about like Hallowe'en masks, and I, who had prided myself that whatever I brought to bear on the project it would not be preconception, was suddenly confronted with the most elementary preconception imaginable. I had brought it with me. It was simply this: when you look at badgers in a book, or on television, or catch one in the beam of car headlights, you see inevitably a hard and recognisable shape in a pool of light. It is as unnatural a representation of a badger as you could conceive. The natural beast, in his natural nocturnal element, does not linger fondly in pools of light. He is a white Hallowe'en mask towing a bulky shadow. To see badgers more accurately, to see them as they are in their preferred night life, you must either develop your natural night sight capabilities (usually unused by humans) to their most astonishing extreme, as Chris Ferris demonstrated in her mesmerising book, *The Darkness is Light Enough*, or be that owl there, looking down.

I am grateful now for that first sight of badgers on their terms. It established at once a new definition of the word 'badger' in my mind, and because it is the true one, it has stayed with me ever since. Every time that I have frozen a badger with my camera's flash, my mind tells me that the light has briefly tricked my eyes. The image is the opposite of sunlight which falls on substance and throws a shadow. In the woodland night, the flash falls on the shadow-creature with the mask and throws a badger.

There is a good compromise, but I did not encounter it for months. By then the conspiracy had taken a kindlier course and I was halfway up a mountain in my own preferred world of the Highland Edge. Before all that, there would be many tribulations.

As I sat under the sycamore I tried to keep track of five Hallowe'en masks and shadows which careered and crashed like the ghosts of dodgem-cars. At times, the badger is as frolicsome as an otter, but I could make little sense of the tumult and its soft yelps and grunts because of the depths of the darkness, and all the time the unnamed unease was at the back of my neck and between my shoulderblades. Even as I crowned my first badger-watching with five rag-tag-and-bobtailing beasts a dozen yards away from where I sat, I wondered why I felt troubled. Ernest Neal wrote that his first encounter was 'a red-letter day in my life as it started me off on a study of these intriguing animals over nearly 50 years ... no occasion has given me more of a thrill than that first introduction to the world of badgers ...' I confess I was not thrilled. That in itself bothered me, because the spectacle of uninhibited nature at close quarters has almost invariably captivated me utterly. Perhaps it was the conspiracy, perhaps the maggoty memory of thirty years ago, perhaps the troubled solitary state of mind. My tape recorder notes for that night included a terse 'It's a slightly claustrophobic world, this, which I don't much care for...' Months later, replaying it, I could hear the tremor of discomfort in the voice.

I spent a late September night alone at home, considering the dilemma in the company of a good whisky. Wildlife and wild places had so often proved to be the enduring solaces of my life, but the more I tried to immerse myself in the badger world of the wood, the more it became immersed in a malaise, a crisis of restlessness which had begun to overwhelm my life. I thought about the other wild theatres I had worked in as a writer – St Kilda, the West Highlands, Glencoe, the Cairngorms, Shetland, Skye, and the wind-and-water-bright world of swans. I moved instinctively through such places but now I had imposed on myself a year in a black and oppressive wood at night. In the process I rediscovered a fear of the dark I had discarded by the time I was ten. I had also turned watching wildlife into a rut, a state of affairs I found unforgiveable.

Each time I set out for the wood I had to turn my back on my Southern Highlands mountain skyline, that Highland Edge which for so long had been my everyday wildlife workplace. If only I could work badgers there, in those woods under the mountains, in touch with my landscape instincts, but the received wisdom was that the old badger population was long gone, the setts overgrown and cold, the badgers hounded out or gassed or both. I had heard it so often, and my own perfunctory explorations seemed to confirm it, but as I drove east once more, I resolved that to do justice to both badgers and myself I would have to change the nature of the project and change it radically. Behind my back, the conspiracy was at work.

'Eight o'clock, completely dark, no sound, only leaves falling, no badgers, only unease at what I'm doing. I have not acclimatised to this place.'

That was my next night's note. That was all.

Late autumn was committed to a series of journeys through Highlands and northern islands, but the Hallowe'en masks were rarely far from my thoughts, and I dissected my notes and tried to make sense of textbooks which seemed to deal in generalities based on southern and midland England. These seemed to bear few similarities with in-dividual circumstances five or six hundred miles further north. I had yet to realise it, but this was my first confrontation with a fundamental badger truth, the capacity of individuals to confound generalities.

I gave the wood one more try. It was early December, ice on the track and a full moon. There was so much light in the surrounding fields and the sky that I approached the wood buoyantly and with a confidence I had not felt since that first August afternoon. Surely the place was not as black as I had painted it in my mind? I entered by the sink, and even forgot to be irritated by it, regarding it rather as an old familiar fragment of the landscape. There were fresh diggings everywhere. Many of them were still wet, and there was fresh dung in the shallow pits and scrapes a few yards from the main sett. Surely the badgers were not out already? It was 3.40 p.m. I crept soundlessly to my accustomed tree on the top of the bank and sat, trying to quieten even the sound of my breathing. As I sat, a shutter fell. No hint of the brimming moonlight reached me or touched the sett, and all my old prejudices reconvened in the instant. Then I heard the blackbirds at work on the owl.

I have known that sound for as long as I can remember. I have admired the relentless purpose of defiance which lies behind it, seen its chisel-on-granite chorus swelled by chaffinches, robins, wrens, even a treecreeper once. Now it put my teeth on edge. As its volume increased and its source grew nearer, I suddenly realised that the birds' attentions had turned from the owl to me. Their secret weapon arrived then, a single magpie. It screeched from four feet above my head, so sudden and so loud that it felt as if I had jumped from a sitting position. Try it sometime. I remembered then my friend Mike Tomkies talking to me darkly about how he had become convinced some kind of malevolent presence was telling him it was time to leave the place where he then lived, a remote cottage on Loch Shiel in the West Highlands. I now sensed the same thing.

I had set out here to become a fragment of the woodland floor, to come close to badgers and learn about them from their midst. Instead I had become of as much account in that woodland as a withered sycamore leaf. Now with the blackbirds and the magpie scolding me, I felt as if nature itself was fashioning a barrier between the badgers and me. This, to a writer whose every instinct and campaigning voice has been dedicated to championing nature's cause, was tough to take.

There will no doubt be those who interpret this as a kind of capitulation to self-pity, but a nature writer working alone is a vulnerable species, hypersensitive to the moods of nature. All your reference points are in nature, and the only assessment of your work and your worth other than your own is your secondary assessment of what nature thinks you are worth. A lot can be lost in that tricky translation! When nature's mood appears to be locked in opposition to your best endeavours, you fall back on your instincts, your principles, your reasons for being there. You cannot question nature, at least not in expectation of anything answering you back. You can only respond to nature as it unfolds in your presence.

I sat making notes until 4.15 p.m., by which time it was too dark to see the white page in my lap. The blackbirds had gone. For three hours more, I sat in the thickening dark, the deepening silence, and nothing stirred. Cold thickened the darkness further. I strained eyes and ears in a ferment of concentration, glaring at the two main sett entrances with such intensity that they started to move, so I switched my eyes off and worked with hearing. Beyond the far sounds of farm and traffic my ears gleaned nothing more than my eyes. In that circumstance, the mind eventually begins to hesitate, then falters, then fails, and you slip below the surface of full consciousness. Twice I dozed off. The first time I resurfaced when an owl yelped yards away. No sooner had the piercing echo of its second syllable faded than the same blanket of sightless soundlessness smothered the wood. The second time I started awake to a scrabbling noise, and convinced in that first waking moment that badgers were all around me, I broke my own rule and snatched up a torch from my pack, pointed it at the sound and lit up the vivid black staring eyes of a field mouse, less than a yard from my right boot. It stood, two-footed for several seconds, doubtless wondering at the sudden moon of the torch, then simply turned and jogged off, unhurried, unperturbed, and my purpose in the wood was in shreds.

3

False Dawn

A BROAD BRUSHSTROKE of fields climbs from the back of the cottage to the skyline, bisected by the curve of a tree-lined loan. It is an illusion. The loan does not really curve, but perspectives and the lie of the land and the way the fields switchback down beyond the skyline to the Firth of Forth tell your eyes there is a curve. The anthem of the place is its winds, for the prevailing westerlies have a free rein across Scotland's lowland waist and smash through the big ash trees on either side of the loan.

I moved into the cottage on Christmas Eve, urged on by affairs of the heart, of nature, and by the conspiracy. I opened the back door late at night and a flock of curlews flew up at the sound. They circled the cottage in the dark and alighted again in the same field almost at once. I felt a spasm of kinship with them, for our winter restlessness had homed in on the same fragment of the land. It is no meagre relationship, to be the kin of curlews.

I had asked my new landlord, a farmer with a lifelong attachment to the ground, a tentative question about badgers. There was good reason to be tentative: wildlife, especially mammal wildlife, has friend and foe in more or less equal numbers among lowland farmers. Badgers? He answered just as tentatively... well, there had been, years ago, but they had been... well, ah, destroyed, well... on wrong advice, he thought now. It seems something had been killing poultry, and he had said fox, but someone knew about a badger sett near the village. Well, no, it had probably been the foxes but the badgers got the blame, although he had disapproved, because didn't your primary school nature study tell you that the badger was the farmer's friend, by and large? Whatever happened to primary school nature study, I wondered, remembering with a long-forgotten affection a raven-haired teacher who overwhelmed my ten-year-old mind one glorious wet Friday and talked enchantingly about kittiwakes and left me walking home on air and free-falling down red sandstone cliffs and flirting loudly with the wind-flicked kisses of the wavetops ...

Where were we? So, he was saying, he hadn't seen a badger here in, oh, ten years – not that he had anything against badgers.

Christmas Day, walking the loan to the skyline, feeling its tree-vaulted avenue with some confidence, a secure landscape lifeline in the midst of that least secure of times. On the skyline its formal avenue aspect ended abruptly and it dipped down almost to the firth as a narrowed and sinuous footpath through smaller trees and thickety holly and bramble. It rose and fell between huge fields, but between these and the shore were two smaller unploughed fields and the footpath degenerated into a small holly-filled glen between two half-hearted burns. Half a mile to the west, on the far side of one of the smaller fields lay a big old wood fringing the shore of the firth.

I looked at the Holly Glen (as it was instantly christened, a good Christmas Day omen) with an appreciative eye and put my embryonic badger store of knowledge to work on it and decided that if the big wood held badgers – it might, it was big enough, open enough and far enough from the farm – then the small fields and the Holly Glen would would be a comfortable night's jaunt and a fruitful foraging ground for earthworms and moles and slugs and the other inhabitants of meadow and leaf-litter not immune to a questing badger snout or that jaw that can take the hand off a man. It would repay a thoughtful exploration.

I was learning, slowly, painstakingly, the hard way, but thankful to be beginning again in a place of buoyant winds, sea-salt scents and big skies fully ten miles from that vile black wood. The wood had exploded one small myth for me, however, for it was clear from the number of mutilated corpses and leftovers around the fringes of the sett that these badgers were considerable devourers of moles. I remembered my Kenneth Grahame again ... 'The Mole had long wanted to make the acquaintance of the Badger...' and decided he could have done with a bit of primary school nature study, except that it probably wouldn't have permitted such an exquisite book to be written.

The day was quiet and wore a sheen of brightening grey. The fields swooped to the firth in unfurling fawn sheets and climbed and fell and climbed again far inland towards low wooded hills. Beneath the sharpest of these hills, a wood crept down a ridge to a dark plantation where badgers lived with robins, and blackbirds hunted in packs, and the moss slowly smothered an old upturned sink. I turned my back on it, symbolically now, and watched the river instead. The Forth is two miles wide here, and in that afternoon light, looked as if a strip of pale jade-shaded silk had been laid across the land. A half-full orangey moon stood low in the sky above the Forth's two mighty bridges, massively outshining their floodlit show, and dousing the river-silk with a bright and almost indefinable shade, a searing grey-blue-yellow-green. The fields mourned, the icy cries of curlew and lapwing. Flocks from handfuls to hundreds drifted to and from the fields and the shore at all hours of the day and half the night, and their cries vied with the shriller pipes of oystercatcher and redshank and small licorice-allsort-headed ringed plovers. All these and many other less familiar wader tribes stabbed and probed and prodded an oozing mesh through mussel-bed and mudflat with an armory of beaks from plover stub to curlew sabre. *This* was a badger realm? At least they would be accustomed to a repertoire of birds more exotically orchestrated than robinsong.

As the thought lodged, a small rustle in a holly bush became a robin, and there it sat and sang, a robin on a holly bush on Christmas Day, and all that night its song was in my ears and from the window beyond my bed rose the soft thin restlessness of curlews like oboe sounds turned to smoke. My own restlessness passed through the glass and mingled with it and I felt, briefly, easier than I had done for years. Perhaps, I told myself, this was what the conspiracy had in mind all along, if only it would turn up badgers on the doorstep as well ...

Now my problems began in earnest. I was about to learn that it is one thing to 'inherit' a watcher's passport to an established and continuously inhabited sett, as I had done in the black wood, and quite another to pin down the home base of badgers tentatively reclaiming a toehold on old haunts from which their forebears had been expunged. Mystery is an integral part of badger-watching when watcher and badger are uncertain of their ground and watching is as much – more – a thing of chance encounter as any planning or routine. But I took to the fields and the scraps of woodland and the brambly bits and the shore with an eagerness which had been quite absent in the black wood, an eagerness fuelled by the open-handed landscape and the joy of discovery, and darkness never troubled me again.

The Holly Glen surpassed itself almost at once. Whatever the shortcomings of my introduction to badger-watching, I now had at least a working knowledge of what a sett looked like, and how to tell a lived-in sett from an abandoned one. Badgers leave clues, blatantly legible clues, and there is no mistaking their message. I had read that, and I had seen it for myself. Alas, it is only half true. There is a great deal of mistaking because there is a great deal of amateur expert theory expounded among even the most casual of badger-watchers. Generalities which take no account of local conditions are delivered in tablets of stone at the first mention of the word 'badger'. I don't know why badgers should attract so many self-styled experts, but I quickly learned not to mention the word unless I was sure of the company I was in. I also learned to junk gratuitous advice completely.

I stepped into the Holly Glen for the first time and found it was carpeted with badger clues. I began to read them carefully.

Badgers dig. They dig for a living, for a home, for worms, slugs, beetles, moles, they dig pits in which to deposit dung (and often miss, it seems to me). They dig from curiosity (a subterranean sound?), and they dig for the hell of it. The Holly Glen was dug. The most spectacular piece of digging was on the lower edge of the glen where it tapered to a small dark corner not far from the shore. The corner was darkened by a Tolkien oak, dour and decrepit and rooted in a mound about four feet high and twice as wide. The mound was holed on two sides and on the top where badgers had made a leaky canopy of the roots. A flattened platform protruding from one side of the mound was the excavated earth worn down by generations of badgers, or so I reasoned. But the main hole was thick with old leaves, and that said the badgers were not in residence. A lived-in sett is meticulously clean, the entrances bare, dug out and brushed out and scoured by the badgers' domestic obsession with a clean floor.

A small open space at the heart of the Holly Glen was scuffed and scraped and pitted and broken open and torn apart, its mosses raked, its tussocks split or overturned. All that is the collective hallmark of badger foraging. Flattened inches-wide paths led up each side of the glen, and one went straight through the densest holly bush, a tunnel eighteen inches high. I passed a hasty verdict on the Holly Glen. It had held badgers at one time but did so no longer. Yet it seemed they came here from somewhere to feed at the very least, perhaps even to hole up for the occasional away day. But away from where? In the first week I had eliminated the big wood to the west, a scruffy and littered labyrinth of cold trails. The nearest sett I knew of was more than a mile away with many a copse and shelter belt and field edge in between; there would simply be no need for a badger from there to forage as far as the Holly Glen.

So now something of the mystery of badgers was beginning to impress itself on me. At least the nature of the mystery, for the more I found or guessed at or suspected, the less became clear. That first week was grey and mild and without a sett to watch, and without the predictability of times and places, I contented myself with walking the ground in daylight, reading the clues, and adding to my list of questions.

There were days when there were no new clues, and that suggested that badgers were not there every night. On other days the ground was slashed and raked and gouged and generally so roughed up that it looked as if a creature halfway between a rogue elephant and a JCB had been at work. Black weals the size of small furrows appeared in the winter leaf-cover, white weals with claw-point tops striped the bark of an ash. Then suddenly an old hole in the field edge next to the Holly Glen was open again and a tell-tale layer of fresh earth door-matted the entrance. On the steep bank of the burn facing the hole was a wide stripe of clawed mud, and on the fence which marks the edge of the Holly Glen was a single hair. It was perhaps two-and-a-half inches long, tipped with white, banded with black then paling to white again. It is the trademark of badger squirming under a fencewire. I picked it up with a glee more appropriate to the discovery of the Holy Grail and carried it home in triumph. One hair among so many straws in the wind. I committed myself to patience, Mole-like, waiting for Badger to turn up.

I told myself that one hair and one opened hole don't amount to a sett on the doorstep, but I was instantly more confident about what I was trying to do than I had been at any time since that dappled afternoon the previous August, aeons ago. It lasted less than forty-eight hours,

On the river below the Holly Glen

Foraging on the woodland floor

A big badger boar makes a track through the wild garlic

Spoil heap, with straw bedding dragged up for an airing

and as far as I know, that hole has not been used since. Still, a badger had turned up and stayed for one short midwinter day, and I sensed that if I hung about the Holly Glen often enough for long enough, I would be able to put the flesh and bones of badgers to that single hair.

At the root of it all was the one essential which is the core of my philosophy concerning wild nature in all its forms from mouse to mountain – the joy of discovery. I preach it as much as I practise it, for there is no substitute for it, but it cannot be faked and it knows no short cut. This badger world to which (as I fancied it) the conspiracy had led me had open skies and wide horizons and the sea sounds of the firth to fill the gaps of the long waits. It might not be perfect but it was getting better.

The worsening weather grew suddenly wild, an unrelenting dirge of sodden westerly gales which roared among the cottage trees. I cowered in the lee of the holly where there was cover of a kind, waiting and watching until it was too cold and too wet to see or think. The badgers snored, warm and dry and God knows where. I went through the whole of January without seeing a badger, but still the clues came and went between gales. I noted them down and gritted my teeth and wondered what the hell to do about it, while a giggling Ratty voice in my head intoned: 'Badger'll turn up some day or other – he's always turning up ... but you must not only take him *as* you find him, but *when* you find him ...'

I thought I had found him in a bank a yard or two above the high tide shingle beach. The banked earth had been carved and smoothed and burrowed, and a clawed ramp climbed one end of it to the footpath above. I sat among the shoreline rocks, dark and slumped as a rock myself. The tide was lapping my boots and the air full of that restlessness of curlews which stirs such an ache of kindred spirit in me. I sat through the early darkness of late afternoons, the middle darkness of late evenings and midnights, the pre-dawn darkness, then the heaviest of rains fell. The bank subsided and redefined itself and all that cut a swathe through all its darknesses were rabbits and mice.

To reach the shore I had to pass the Holly Glen, so each time I passed I would pause to scan the page of each new day for badger scribblings. It was more or less as I was giving up on the shore that two more clues surfaced at the Holly Glen, bolstering instinct, inclining me back towards that sloping, tapering wedge of dark winter green. If there was a resident badger population (see how I had begun to punctuate with ifs and buts – I never did lose that habit with badgers, being more impressed with their mysteries than the few certainties) I was at last beginning to believe that the glen was a pivotal part of its landscape.

The first new clue was the discovery that the three badger-fashioned paths in the glen – one up each side, one through the middle of the central mass of holly, a bottle-green tunnel – met at the top of its small hill and entered and left the glen as one. From there, that deeper-imprinted path reached into the bottom of the loan before turning at right-angles under a fence, then away west by a field edge, growing indistinct. There too, on the bottom fence wire, was a small broomful of badger hairs. I removed these carefully and leaned three twigs against the wire like a wicket on the path. If it was a regular badger route they would knock the twigs aside and more hairs would snag the fence. I could stake out the crossing and learn.

The second clue, when it eventually turned up, was a telling part of the learning. Next day, the sticks were down, and the next, and as often as I replaced them after that they were down within a day or two, usually one. From time to time there was a badger hair or two on the wire. Reset the sticks, clean off the hairs, and learn. In this way I kept watch on the shore a week more and kept a kind of shorthand note on the Holly Glen and the crossing which seemed to be the glen's main entrance. All the while the shore stayed badgerless as the sticks skittled over up at the crossing with heartening regularity. I gave up shore-watching and started crossing-watching. But when to watch? The times badgers emerge from their setts and the reasons for the times, the changing pattern of the times and the inexplicable lapses among the patterns are the stuff of a verbose mass of expert theory. I consulted Ernest Neal's truly expert and un-verbose monograph, but there was little that made sense in 'average' emergence timetables relative to sunset in the south of England, and I added latitude to the experts' in-exhaustible list of variables.

It had become ever more clear to me that I was dealing with a tribe of individuals. The whims and wiles of individualists have a propensity for making a mockery of received wisdom. I discarded theories as fast as I invented them, and admired badgers the more for their indifference to my efforts to make sense of them. I was never closer to reneging on my pledge to myself and going back to one of my handed-on-a-plate setts a few miles to the south, and as I confronted the problem of watching the crossing, I cursed my own perversity more than once.

The problem was this: when to watch not knowing where the sett was, nor when the badgers emerged from it, nor how much longer before they left its vicinity to forage, nor how long it might take them to travel however far it might be . . .

It was my third evening watching the crossing, mid-March, a low ground mist lying on the field bottom, a skimpy, half-hearted waist-high mist. I had begun by watching from 6 to 9 p.m., then 7 to 10 p.m., and now I was working the 8 to 11 shift. By ten o'clock the folds of the land were unfathomably black, but always the firth and its small shore towns and sky-reflected Edinburgh, just out of sight to the east, put enough light about the fields to walk safely without the need of a torch. I sat above the crossing on top of a small bank, the wind pushing my scent away east, the badger path approaching downwind. The mist shifted in that black and pale night, and at times it caught the reflected light and orangey wafts of it would bend into reptilian shapes, but the shadowed places held it black and still and thick as treacle. It lay something lighter than treacle and duller than orange along the last shoreward slopes of the big fields above the Holly Glen, a translucent lemon grey when the moon touched it.

I had been watching it for more than an hour. It is a difficult thing to do, concentrating on mist where there are no focal points. I locked on to where I fancied the extended line of the crossing path burrowed into the mist. Keeping my head still, I let my eyes work through narrow arcs to each side. If the badgers which were using the crossing and the Holly Glen were not coming from that direction, then they were wilier and I was more obtuse than I had imagined. The close call of an owl or mouse-rustle at my back might jerk my head free, but I tried to resist such things. What I had come to see can appear and disappear in the space of a blink, and a mouse in the sights of a diverted glance would be a poor consolation if I missed the badger.

In that prime spell of the watching, every sense strains for messages and only sight is handicapped. So I first sensed then heard and finally saw the badger shambling his way to the field edge. His swaying rum-te-tum walk shouldered a furrow through the mist, white face nodding like a plough-harnessed Clydesdale. He was head-down, pausing often to listen, and looked as preoccupied as Pooh. At ten feet away from the crossing when it seemed he must trundle straight to the fence, squirm under it, scattering my sticks and giving me the picture I had so painstakingly set up, he bounded left, shot through the hedge (a gap unknown to me) into the bottom field with a startling turn of speed. The night offered no further hint that he had ever been.

It was the first time I had seen a badger run, and even for the shadow of a shroud at the edge of reliable night vision it was an impressive sight. There was also a hint of rising up out of his low-slung walking gait like an inflating hovercraft, the surge forward at speed the work of a body not quite in contact with the ground. It was one of those characteristic punctuations of all my badgering endeavours south of the Forth which promised much but delivered more frustration than fulfilment.

I sat through another empty and chilling hour with my camera primed for that precise shot which the badger had so nearly provided. I had been denied it by some flaw of my own no doubt, a trivial movement like the brush of a jacket cord perhaps, just enough to convey an implied threat to the badger. At first he would have seen only the dark shape and come on, curious, in the manner of all weasels (to which tribe – the *mustelae* – he rightly belongs). Sight is the sense he relies on least, and he would want a scent or a sound from the shadow. He got what he wanted, all the warning required to bolt for cover, perhaps to that burnside hole in the bottom field where he would have to barge through two more of my sticks. As I waited, I sensed him there, deep in the dark earth, facing the entrance, holding his curiosity in check, waiting himself for instinct to urge him on again, perhaps to the Holly Glen by way of a clawed scramble up the burn bank and under the fence, catching another neck hair on the bottom wire and leaving it there for me to find in the morning. I duly found it.

I waited on another hour for no good reason, slave to my own instincts of stillness and patience. The river slapped up the shingle and sucked back down it. Owls conversed over the heads of the big trees. Lapwings moaned in the high fields where they stood through the darkness of the high tide hours, lifted stiffly in small slow squadrons to glide a dozen yards to a new stance, restless too as any curlew flock. The third hour was one of the coldest I ever spent at the badgers, and I abandoned it when uncontrollable shivering ended any serious prospects of staying still enough to do the job.

Walking home, stiffer than a gliding lapwing, a slow trudge up the steepest of the fields' switchbacks, weighing up the evening, wondering just how far west the sett really was and whether or not it was near enough to be an element of what I had already fondly defined as my territory, I saw again what may well have been the same badger, just as it swayed in on the dozing lapwing flock. Often I had imagined such an encounter. The lapwings would lift in a reflex action of deference to that swaying, padding, nodding night march of the badger, watching him pass ten feet below the stiff stretch of their wings. I had not envisaged, however, that one bird should succumb to the temptation of a swooping dare, inches above the badger's unflinching head. This higher, open brow of the field was a better lit stage than the dark folds by the crossing, but still a theatre of shadows, so that the quality of the bird's daring was subdued. But I saw the pale breast of the bird detach from the gliding squadron and dart down, flailed by its own shadow of wings, saw it mask for a second the pale badger head as it danced close, saw it spring up palely again, saw the badger head thrust on, low to the ground, nodding its perpetual affirmative, the bird of no more account than a moth. A lapwing about your head, it said, is nothing more than confirmation of your supremacy over lapwings.

Besides, there were more pressing concerns. I had turned aside, further out into the field, to come below the lapwing flock and minimise my disturbance of their night, and ensured unwittingly that my path would be crossed by the badger's. Now his nose was to the fresh man-scent of my diversion. It clearly consumed his every attention and energy, and all his concerns. It would tell him (I guessed, for who *really* knows who is not a badger?) that I had passed very recently. He would know too that I was moving too slowly to have travelled far. (This is a particularly reasonable guess on my part: if I, a badger-watching novice, can tell from a set of badger tracks whether the beast was sitting, standing, scrambling, loping or running, how much more fluent must the badger be with the tracks of man, the one scent in the aeons of his evolution he ever had cause to fear, the one enemy on the face of the land.) So in his mind I was nearby and a threat.

He stopped, sat back on his haunches and listened, peering through a web of shadows. I stood among them, close by the trees again having rounded the lapwings, above him, perhaps twenty yards away. He seemed to look straight at me for what felt like minutes but was probably only a handful of long seconds. Then his eyes drifted on. As he sat, the impatient lapwing reared again, high enough this time for me to see its perfect crested silhouette and dangling legs against the sky over the firth. It fell at the badger's head, so close that a turn and a snap would have ended its foolish life. The badger head watched and listened and scented among the shadows and the air currents; to him the lapwing was just a flickering fragment of the night.

The movement forward of a sitting badger from hunkers to all-fours is one of the most bear-like gestures he makes. Watching him, small in the open widths of field and firth and sky and night, I thrilled to a badger for the first time. I felt a compulsive edge about the quest I had set myself. In that single gesture my work was handed the impetus it had needed. I stood enthralled as the badger put its nose to my trail and came on, bear-bold, weasel-curious.

Three times in the twenty meandering yards between the point at which he stood and the point where I stood commanding my very best stillness to perform to its utmost, the badger sat three times and listened and tasted the air on his nose. Three times he stood, bear-like, and came on. He was perhaps six feet away from me when he stopped for a fourth time and detected my shadow, or rather the meaning behind my shadow. He gave a soft, questioning grunt, turned in his own length and walked away down the field. *Walked!*

I stood, as rooted as the holly at my back, while his bear-gait and broad beam dwindled methodically down the field. Once he stopped and looked back, half turned, and I willed him back, but he turned again and took to the very edge of the field where I lost him in the shadows and the mist.

I would have called a halt to the whole thing there and then. How could I improve on that? I suddenly knew I didn't want to get so familiar with badgers that I took them for granted, the way many a habitual badger-watcher can tell you that at certain times of the year at certain setts they can set their watch by the badger's habits. I had met this badger by luck, but luck which I had made by way of painstaking effort. Yet I was still no nearer to knowing where it came from or where it went. By reading the first of those clues on the ground by the Holly Glen and putting to work that little gleaning of knowledge which had begun to infiltrate the bliss of my ignorance, I had established the glen as a reliable point of contact. If I watched the place often enough I would certainly see badgers on occasion, but would I too learn to set my watch by their appearance? The idea suddenly appalled me. Instead I felt the need to meet the badger out in his world, to learn what his world looked like, and felt like, to meet his fellow travellers – like the lapwing – to put in my mind a painting, not a literal thing like a Landseer or a Thorburn, but an impressionist account of the badger world, blurred and coloured by my writer's brushstrokes, but based on a sure drawing. I felt finally vindicated in turning my back on the inland setts I was first shown the previous summer.

With that I strode happily down the far side of the fields to the welcoming lit square of the cottage window, blind for the moment to the shadow of the conspiracy which had not done with me yet.

Between the unfolding of the first of the Holly Glen's clues and the second, another factor infiltrated the conspiracy's scheme of things and began almost at once to undermine that most promising phase of my badger endeavours and show it for something of a false dawn. As the idea of examining the wider badger world rooted within me and I began to explore its possibilities, a missing ingredient presented itself. Mountains.

4

Spring of Hope

ONE MARCH NOON, walking alone over the fields to the Holly Glen, feeling the year's first clear sun sharp on my face, relishing the lull between storms, I was accompanied by the blunt and russet flight of a pair of partridges and the slurping, syrupy kisses of their calls. Partridges in various numbers had been amiable and constant company on any walk over the fields, confiding voices of the dawn and the dusk and the dark. Now it looked as if this pair had detached from the whirring flocks of winter and were territorially inclined. I hoped they might nest in the edge of the loan and avoid the neighbourhood sparrowhawks.

I crossed the summit of the fields with the partridges in tow to encounter for the first time there a day of almost limitless visibility. There, a blue taunt, were the mountains of my Southern Highlands skyline. They looked distorted in their familiarity by an extreme easterly perspective, and diminished by distance. I stopped and stared and felt a stab of pain, the pain of deprivation.

It also proved to be a galvanising pain. I acknowledged at once that those mountains had been too important a part of my life for too long to turn my back on them. I did not want to be without them. Almost in the same breath of awareness I began to wonder if I could extend my badger work to its wider world, encompassing my own landscape preferences. It was true that every conversation I could recall with sundry wildlife experts and enthusiasts along the Highland Edge insisted that badgers were long gone, like its corncrakes and its golden eagles. Yet wildlife regimes change and evolve. The conditions for corncrakes and eagles had gone, probably changed irrevocably, but there was still suitable badger habitat. With that troublesome 'if only ...' preoccupying me, I came down to the crossing above the Holly Glen.

I reset the scattered sticks, clambered the fence, cursed holly and bramble, and reached the small clearing which is the heart of that place. For the second time in an hour I stopped in my tracks and stared. The floor of the clearing was a shambles of furrowing and digging. Grasses were uprooted and piled and dragged. Small branches were smashed. Everywhere lay the littered evidence of a considerable mayhem. A couple of yards from where I stood was a hole, a new hole with a newly excavated spoilheap, the doormat hallmark of badgers. Nearby a dollop of fresh dung shone wetly in its small pit. I marvelled at that grey-brown nugget as if it had been gold.

Suddenly I was the focal point of crazily competing forces. Moments before I had succumbed to the temptation of a beckoning mountain vision. Now I was presented with the most persuasive of nature's gestures to resist the mountain siren-song. Nature had brought me badgers. The mountain had come to Mohammed and camped practically in his back garden.

Then a third voice made itself heard. It was the measured reasoning voice of the naturalist. A badger has been here, it said. It has even excavated a small and probably temporary hole and defecated nearby. That is no more a permanently occupied sett than a swallow makes a summer, though it is a good reason for putting in a lot more work.

I was elation and caution in the same breath. Then, as if to underscore nature's intentions for me, a robin stepped up from the edge of the hole to the holly tree and sang. I sat and listened, and I told him aloud 'I hear you, I hear you', and in my mind I was fifteen again and felt the deadweight of the old broken boar, and the darker side of me, competing to be heard above the blithe robinsong, wondered if that was to be the role of badgers in my life forever, a deadweight.

If only I had not let the Highland Edge into the reckoning, if only I had not so recently determined to consider the whole wider world of badgers, I could have miniaturised their world down to this single triangular acre, become an element in it night after night so that they would expect to find me by the big ash as they would expect to find moles and earthworms, beetles and slugs, holly and the sounds of the trickling burns and the river sucking at its rock shore. Even as I turned

41

the idea over, I realised that I had passed that point. This had been my proving ground and it had served me well, but I had let Highland light and wilder air into the holly-dark wedge.

What if badgers did re-establish here? They might fare none too well at the hands of the farm, or the 'terrier boys'. It would take only the sight of a badger crossing a field full of cattle in broad daylight to re-awaken old and barely slumbering warhorses like the bovine TB scare. Such laws as there are to protect badgers are powerless against determined individuals at night. More than one seasoned badger watcher cautioned against tangling with such people if I encountered them. One put it:

'If a badger can't handle what they throw at him on his own ground in the dark, you sure as hell can't.'

A voice hailed me from the field, none too pleasantly, then changed to apologetic recognition. It was the farmer.

'Oh, it's you. I didn't recognise you. I was down the field there after a yowe and I saw movement and thought it was another beast maybe.' He nodded at my binoculars. 'Birdwatching is it?'

It was the first time I'd been mistaken for a yowe. I told him reluctantly about the badgers. It was his land, and he'd have to know sometime or other.

'Badgers! No, no, you're mistaken. Not here. Maybe in the big wood yonder, but not here, not for years now.'

As he spoke the wet dung of the night before was perhaps twenty yards from his right boot. I changed the subject to the shelduck which I could see massing boldly and beautifully behind his back.

'Aye, they're pests, after the barley...' and at that he launched into a ramble about the trials of being a farmer, which as far as I could see were so all-embracing and terminal that he could only resolve his difficulties by not farming in the countryside. He left with his yowe and I turned my thoughts away from badgers to the spectacle which grew by the moment in his field. The shelduck is a handsome exotic, lording it over the mud-colour tribes of shoreline waders, more goose than duck, erect as a greylag, bottle-green-headed, scarlet-nebbed (embellished in the male by a circular growth like a glass bottle stopper), black and white body distinguished by a vivid chestnut scarf echoed by a wing-feather wedge of the same shade. In the space where the farmer had stood obscuring my view of the field, forty-two of these preposterous creatures strung an unforgettable furrow across the field, trampling and nibbling barley shoots as they advanced uphill, a platoon as raggedly disciplined as they were supremely uniformed. Pests? Perhaps, but only if yours was the wallet which paid for the barley.

All afternoon, as the tide flowed and the mudflats dwindled, a fawn rain fell on the fields. Flocks of curlews lifted up from the shore and gained just enough height to glide flatly down on upheld down-curved wings. Between four and five hundred now stood in a thick circle, completely surrounding the shelduck like redskins round a wagon train.

Walking the field by the loan I saw the sparrowhawk male soar up, treetop high, then dive down through the trees to cross the loan at grass-top height and fly fast and straight uphill ahead of me. Almost at once there was a speckle of feathers on the ground at my feet, then a few yards further on the headless corpse of a partridge, the blood still flowing, the body still warm but cooling. It is the hawk's way with a kill, that headlessness.

I needed (I thought, for the last time, as it happened) the help of a more experienced point of view on the circumstances of the Holly Glen's new badger hole. I needed to know quickly whether or not I should pour time and energy into watching it. I made a phone call.

'Nursery sett, a sow with cubs almost certainly. You're getting lucky at last,' came the music to my ears. But the cautionary instincts, which had grown perceptibly since I had begun to watch badgers, counselled a sage 'beware' and a second opinion. I got it.

'Probably nothing more than an old boar on his own. He probably won't stay.'

Experts? I decided to watch anyway. The sow-and-cubs theorist had added the rider that I should tread extra warily. Don't go too near too soon. Keep at least twenty yards back to be safe. But twenty yards back would put me ten yards into the fields on either side or deep in the prickle-thick heart of a great and gloomy density of holly shrubbery. By 7 p.m. I was twenty feet away, my back to a huge beech, starting again, a fragment of the woodland floor again, preaching patience to myself again, re-learning stillness (which you must practise constantly, nursing it like a good golf swing, to be any good at it), still as that partridge up the field. I sat with the wind whistling away my scent to the shore, tape recorder primed, camera in hand, waiting.

An hour-and-a-half later, my optism had slipped into neutral and I was dreaming of mountains.

Yet still I waited, and while my eyes wandered off from the badger hole for light relief I saw a pheasant fly down from a wall and begin to cross the bottom field, goose-stepping towards the glen, hiccuping absurdly at every other step, until it had hiccuped to the edge of the burn below me and flew, up a vertical cacophonous shaft of air, up into an ash to roost. It did not land in the tree so much as subside, perched among the topmost branches, nature's weathercock. For thirty minutes more the west wood echoed as its eastmost treetops sprouted a dozen weathercocks.

Badger-watching, I now know, is a human perversity. Not only is it predatory on domestic and social life as most humans know them, it practises excruciating forms of discomfort: either it is too cold to sit still for more than two hours at a time, or, when it is warm enough to sit still indefinitely, badger setts support intensive breeding programmes for midges, and it is impossible to be still for two minutes at a time. As soon as the midges fade with earliest autumn, the first frosts materialise and you remember what it is like to shiver again. And most of the time it's dark anyway.

Cold gripped the Holly Glen in the last half hour of my vigil. I waited on through it buoyed only by the near-certainty (an unreliable state of affairs in a naturalist) that I had seen a wavering badger head just inside the hole. The wavering, I would learn, is typical, for the badger likes to greet the overworld cautiously, testing and tasting the air for unsavoury scents for minutes at a time, then unaccountably withdrawing again. If the scent *is* unsavoury, that's it for hours, or the whole night; if it suggests all is well, the badger will hang about just out of sight in the burrow for just long enough to drive the badger-watcher into a silent frenzy of heightened expectation. The particular circumstances of this night by this hole were such that I had convinced myself at least one badger would emerge and so complete a cycle of endeavour. I even leaned fondly towards the sow-with-cubs theory, for it was the quietest piece of ground I knew of in the local landscape which was also suitable for badgers. Optimism had me, even in that last shivering half hour, but despite the vision of the wavering badger head, no badger showed.

Cold finally overcame my reluctance to leave and my optimism turned to ice. The fifteen-minute walk over the hill to the cottage was a black mile, one of the blackest I ever walked, but before I left I put sticks across the hole, and in the morning I would go back that one more time it invariably takes if you would work with nature on nature's terms.

In fact there would be several one-more-times, for although the sticks were undisturbed in the morning, they were knocked over when I checked again two days later, but as far as I can tell, the sett was not used again. Badgers still go in about the Holly Glen, but they live somewhere else, and by midsummer they no longer used the crossing place.

Besides, instinct – and not much else – was urging me back towards the Highland Edge. More and more I had come to think of the badger as a freewheeler, an individualist. I wanted to know that side of his character, the solitary wanderer plotting his way wild and free across the landscape of the dusk. I also wanted to watch him in a better landscape than this, one where the woodlands and lochs, foothills and skyline mountains have been lifelines to me for half my life. By way of extra incentive to return to the Highland Edge, a pivotal day in my wildlife year was nearing.

Something around the first week of April an absented silhouette reappears, dipping downwind towards a small group of massive 150-feet-high firs. The shape hangs, looking down, supreme worker of the wind, fluent as kestrels. It edges sideways from treetop to treetop, testing memory. It is looking for something like a beaver lodge in the sky, or as much of it as the winter storms have left. But it has been a dire winter of all but ceaseless storm. There is nothing left, not so much as a stick, although around the base of the eastmost tree is a great litter of broken branches, smashed and splintered by their fall.

The ritual of nature which is the spring return of the osprey is a phenomenon. The male bird arrives a few days before his mate, barging up the globe from Africa to swap equatorial suns for Scottish springs and Highland winter hangovers. For twenty successive springs I have greeted him from the stony shore of a nearby loch, often with his head-down hover-hunting silhouette pinned against a far mountain backcloth. It was the first week of April again. The twenty-first spring beckoned.

There are always false starts, big gulls and herons mostly, sometimes a buzzard, but only the osprey hovers over the water, and at once you remember again the detail of its distinctive flight, and the first glimpse turns a key in the wild year, and unlocks a hoard of memories. There were the early days of through-the-night watches in a flimsy, leaky tent armed with spotlight and megaphone to fend off intruders (they were used twice and actually worked!); an anxious 3 a.m. alarm call to the police when repeated car engine sounds suggested a vehicle stuck in the osprey wood – I feared the worst but it turned out to be a passing car rally. Then an RAF helicopter ferried in a hide for us, lowered it in sections into a woodland clearing from which it was manhandled through a plantation and assembled. The ospreys gave us one year's use of it then moved trees. The hide is still where we left it, rotting quietly, contemplating a dead pine and being pissed on by passing foxes.

There are a thousand images of the birds fishing, as spectacular a Highland showpiece as eagles displaying or the red deer rut. Most vivid of these images is a huge female, fresh from Africa, shouldering her way through a blizzard twenty feet from my lochside stance with a three-pounder thrashing in her feet. She appeared as a wraith, became substance, then wraith again as she hurdled up over the shoreline trees.

The waiting, which is my purpose on the shore, can be days, hours if you are lucky, minutes, this memorable year, for I was no sooner seated as comfortably as the rooted rocky shore allows and scouring the sky and the old known perching trees, when I became aware of the osprey out in the middle of the loch and heading purposefully towards the shore. He passed fifty yards to my right climbing gradually up an 80-feet-high ramp of air which just cleared the shoreline trees, the trout twitching in his two-footed life-crushing clasp.

I say I 'became aware' of the osprey, and here I acknowledge a phenonemon of osprey-watching. I have heard others ascribe something similar to eagles and otters. The watcher's mind is locked into the dome of sky and its bird shapes. The mind is focussed on that airy terrain, trying to divine an osprey shape there, homed in on that single idea to the exclusion of everything else. You can try no harder, concentrate no more powerfully. Then suddenly the osprey shape you are seeking is in the middle of the sky and flying towards you and you never saw how it got there. It has happened to me a hundred times before and I am no closer to fathoming the mystery of it: how a bird with a five or six feet wingspan and a singularly distinctive way of flying and a spectacular way of fishing can materialise in the middle of the sky with its fish caught.

He crossed the shoreline trees with the sun on him and his glittering prize, heading for a perch near the eyrie tree half-a-mile deep into the woods.

The soft option on such a cool spring day is to drive half a parallel mile to a wide and worn piece of roadside verge and by the time you put the glasses on the skyline trees the osprey should be there. The osprey was not there, and the most cursory glance through the glasses explained why he was not there. There was no eyrie in the eyrie tree.

That winter of storms which had so inhibited my badger-watching had lifted last year's eyrie out of its massive 150-feet treetop and scattered it about the roots of the woodland floor. It was no meagre achievement for a wind either, for the eyrie had developed storey by storey over four or five years since the last great winter gale had cleared it out. So what was felled was a solid plug of broken branches compacted by its own vast weight and measuring perhaps eight feet across and possibly twice as deep. The eyrie had filled a gap between the twin spires of the treetop. Now the spires stood tall and unencumbered, and the shape of the tree was transformed and looked young again.

The tree is one of a group of eight giants towering over the wood, and planted during the early Victorian heyday of estates like this. The heyday is long gone, of course, and the woodland grows slowly down at heel, the breathy spaces among the trees choked now with rampant rhododendrons and bracken. The ground-floor wildlife dwindles in the process although the branches teem with birds.

The eight giants are an exclusive cabal, a brotherhood of woody sages exchanging lofty truths in a parliament of perpetual winds. How often have I watched from the shelter of the roots while the icy gales of what passes for spring on the Highland Edge screeched at the eight for the way they impede the wind's barnstorming march across the the top of the wood? On such a day, when the female osprey may be laying her clutch of two or three, she will feel her chosen nursery sway, the whole mass moving five or six feet through the air. The bird is unmoved by the gale, though. She has confidence in the building, for the eyrie is constructed with just such a wind in mind, repaired and shored and buttressed and strengthened continuously. The tree is chosen not just for its unhampered prospects in every direction, but for its supple strength, for its way of giving, but not giving in, before such a wind. Besides, why should high airy movement trouble a sitting bird which is the essence of flight itself? If you or I perched there in such a wind, we would cling for dear life, yet the male eases down the turbulence to perch precisely on the female's back, mates with her, steps off and drifts a knot above stalling speed to the next tree and grooms himself one-footed. Or perhaps he alights two trees to the west where, on the topmost curve of the topmost branch of the tallest tree of all, he will pin the fish in his foot to the branch and, precisely balanced, begin to eat while she screeches thinly at him from the eyrie for her share. Ospreys fly in the face of ocean winds if the migratory urge compels them. These treetop winds we may call gales are of no account, save that now and again during the osprey-less winters, they re-arrange the furniture.

So I had driven my soft-option half-mile and now considered the empty tree and its empty sky. Should I tramp the woods and watch from closer in and see if I could gather some scrap of knowledge, some indication of the bird's intent? Or should I give him a few days' grace by which time his mate would have arrived and they would have come to their own conclusions and acted on them? I chose a compromise. It was too soon to go and I had seen too little of the osprey and had too little of my curiosity satisfied. I would not walk into the heart of the wood but to a brackeny bank that rises above a burn and forms a boundary for the wood. The burn is flat and straight here, half an undeviating mile, the colour of a good Glenlivet, with the wood on one side and open ground on the other. This open ground gathers itself into the flattened dome of the bank fifty feet above the burn and a hundred yards to the north of it. The bank is an old haunt, commanding a huge swathe of sky, an unrivalled viewing point for the aerobatics of ospreys and buzzards and the more mundane flights of all the lesser fowl of the wood. Roe deer ghost along both sides of the burn, crossing by their own muddy ramps down and up its near vertical banks, dismissive of a plank bridge nearby.

The grey-brown ghost on the bank was the roe doe, her coat in the last of its winter shades, but her flanks showed where a bramble thorn or a birch twig had cut through to the vivid summer chestnut beneath. She was very pregnant and twice as wary as normal, and even her normal is outstanding. She saw me (and probably heard and smelled me) before I saw her, but I marked the careful nature of her retreat, stepping away up a diagonal track of her own making to the screening trees – hawthorn, birch, sycamore, a few rogue spruces boldly breaking ranks from the plantation behind the bank. There she would stand and watch, assessing my threat, so I gave her peace and detoured far and wide to the east. The detour took me up through the middle of the bank by a small hawthorn where another trail through the old bracken was wider and flatter than a roe deer was likely to lay down. It was only vaguely puzzling, for my head was full of roe and osprey, and I almost failed to notice the re-entry of the conspiracy. A side-glance caught a dip in the face of the bank and the lip of a spillage of fresh earth, and with two long uphill strides I was looking down on the biggest badger hole I have ever seen before or since.

An instinct of submerged memory surfaced. Three or four years before, I had found this hole, found it old and cold and cobwebbed. I mentioned it to a badger-thirled friend and forgot about it, assisted by his assurance that it had been ten years since badgers had been seen hereabouts. He knew another sett on the far side of the wood where he'd watched them and found the grizzly aftermath of the gassing.

'I know who did it,' he has told me often, the revenge unsatisfied, 'for there was a cigarette end there and only one man smokes these particular cigarettes round here.'

He put a name to the criminal and I knew it too for he once nailed a couple of harrier wings to a post and was doubtless paid for doing so. There are those – good naturalists as often as not – instinctive countrymen who see the land and its creatures only as a means to a living, stealthy and skilful killers usually, and if someone wants a badger sett stilled they know how to get hold of such a skill. The badger-gasser and harrier-nailer was a hired assassin, nothing less, but good at it, and proving it was all but impossible.

What I remembered of this hole was something about a third of what I now found. A shelf of spoil had been newly dug out on to the brackeny slope, and the tunnel (as vast as the hole) was clean and clear and said 'badger' in its every hallmark.

I heard a familiar sound at my back, a thin rising crescendo of high-pitched cries, the alarm call of ospreys, but closer and louder, much louder than I had heard it before. I turned, startled, from the badger hole to confront an extraordinary sight, the male osprey in flat-out low and level flight not 20 yards away and aimed straight at my head. The instant I turned, the bird dipped a wing, veered and climbed. The air through his wings was the fine rasp of swordplay slashing through winds. I am as sure as I can be that the bird would have come no closer even if I had not turned. I was also uncomfortably aware that, although I was fully a quarter of a mile from the nest and had never elicited alarm calls before from the distance of this bank, there could be no mistaking the specific nature of the protest nor the lengths to which the osprey had gone to deliver it. At once I found myself wishing I had seen the whole gesture, the total protest from beginning to end.

The osprey circled my stance once, head-down, watching. I wondered briefly how all that must look to a surfacing fish eye, staring fearfully up.

Now there were other sources of discomfort for the osprey. That single sun-wise circle ended abruptly in a powerful climb at the top of which was a cruising buzzard. The buzzard saw him coming and fell to meet him, and so began several minutes of aerial high jinks as thrilling as they were pointless. Buzzard and osprey expend endless energies in these jousts, tumbling, cart-wheeling, side-slipping out of fast collision courses, turning talon to talon, flying break-neck-fast and wingtip-close. They are perfectly matched combatants but I never yet saw either bird land a blow. They seem to establish nothing over one another and deliver only mutual protest. They complete only for airspace, for the osprey is exclusively an eater of fish, which a buzzard does not know how to catch, or to carry, or even to eat.

On the top of the bank I watched the birds finally break off and resume their more purposeful nesting season duties. I thought about the prospect which had so suddenly presented itself – badgers, ospreys and buzzards in the same territory. I could only conclude (on the basis of the adversity which had attended my badger work so far) that the conspiracy had briefly taken leave of its senses and that nature would quickly contrive to undermine the opportunity it had just created. But for a while, an hour or two, it tantalised me, and I saw summer cubs about my feet and fledgling ospreys carving airy spirals high overhead, the badgers cocking an ear to their far-carrying cries. The stuff of dreams.

5

The Grapevine

I NSTINCT ASSERTS ITSELF swiftly in any sustained study of nature. I learned years ago to trust it utterly. If it is a well founded instinct and well maintained by constant use, it is all but flawless. In the bank by the osprey wood it pronounced that here was a badger presence in much the same category as the Holly Glen – an outpost, a bolt-hole, an occasional residence. There were none of the characteristics of a well used sett. Judging by the freshness of the small spoil heap and the swept clean entrance, it had been used recently. Even if it was no longer occupied, the hole was evidence at least of a badger presence in a landscape where local opinion held there had been none for ten years.

Could it be that something had changed?

Could it be that the received wisdom had missed the change because it had grown stale and cold, innured by years of badger failure? Vigilance flags in such circumstance. Enthusiasm wanes. Received wisdom grows out of date but remains currency.

I spent the rest of the daylight criss-crossing the bank, and its flat top and sloping flanks. Tracks led to and from the hole on to the top of the bank where they grew indistinct and dissipated among all the symptoms of badger foraging – diggings, rakings, grass-flattenings. There was something else: three or four small patches of bare earth had been worn clear of grass and bracken and now grew a thick crop of shed badger hairs. Not just the neck and back hairs which I recognised at once having plucked them so triumphantly from the Holly Glen fence but also mats of dark underfur. Here, I concluded, was where a badger or badgers were accustomed to sit and scratch, presumably as they began to moult.

Accustomed. The word stuck in my head, lodged like a thorn in a badger foot. How accustomed? How long? How long does it take for a badger to wear a patch of bracken and grass to the bare earth just by sitting on it? And if this was the occasional resort of a single badger, how long to wear out four patches? Had there been badgers here all winter?

I considered the possibilities on that early April evening from the cool brow of the small bank. The osprey wood was an obvious choice, a wide and deep mix of every shape and shade of woodland, mostly undisturbed. With rough grazing fields nearby, it was ideal for badger foraging. I would have to explore it, although like the black Lothian wood where I first watched badgers, the prospect did not enthral me. What did appeal was the second possibility. Perhaps I had found not a high outpost from the low-lying woodland but a low outpost from a hillside sett to the north.

This landscape climbs in three leaps: woodland to bank, a skip of fifty feet; bank to foothills, a bound of anything up to a thousand feet; foothills to mountainside, an elevation to a different realm three thousand feet above the wood. What tantalised me was the possibility of a connecting thread of badger communication from woodland to mountain, an unbroken chain of badger tracks moving through all the elements of the Highland Edge, climbing as I had myself climbed countless times from the osprey wood to the treeline at 1,800 feet and on to the open mountain. All that was against the idea was what I, like everyone else, had assumed to be the total absence of badgers.

I sat on the bank and turned to look south over the low trees to the giants lording it over the skyline and to that distant silhouette on the topmost branches, a small, slender and erect shape, the male osprey at ease, homeless for these one or two pivotal days of his year before the nest-building would begin again. Then, looking north, up through the darkening foothill folds to the piled tiers of mountain shapelessness behind, such a familiar clutch of landscape stepping stones in my eye, I saw it all as if I had never seen it before. For now I looked with a badger's eye. I was a threading badger, seeking out the stepping stones of the landscape's floor, fashioning alleyways and causeways, underground and overground, through copse and cairn and over burn and boulder, between the hole halfway down the bank between my feet and that high silver rock which marks the spot where the mountain moved at the end of the winter.

It was an uncanny idea in every aspect of its rash hypothesis, the more uncanny because in its every aspect it came true.

There is, among the handful of people who work for wildlife or the environment in an area like that compact arc of the Highland Edge, something of a grapevine. It is a subliminal thing, sometimes protectionist, sometimes generous with time or advice or practical assistance (the loan of a boat, a book, a tape recorder) or, more rarely, with information. Still more rarely, if you put a seed of new information into the informal pool of expertise which the grapevine encompasses, it bears remarkable fruit. The whole thing functions informally, is more or less immune to abuse, yet is almost unaware of itself as an entity. It does not meet, for example, ever. You cannot make a phone call and ask someone to put the word around. But if you pass on something you have learned to a listening ear in the bar under the mountain, it can travel 20 miles and reach half a dozen more ears before you get home. I now confided in just such an ear about the hole in the bank and found myself rewarded at once with details of old badger haunts before they had – more or less mysteriously – drifted away from those setts all across the landscape from which they had not been forcibly removed.

The ear knew what it was talking about, a lifelong badger-watcher and one with an intimate knowledge of the Highland Edge. He had never known of a sett in the bank but he had long suspected another sett lay deep in the osprey wood. He thought perhaps they had clung furtively on deep in that dark and untrampled place. He had searched often when his home sett to the south of the wood was sabotaged, years back, but he had never been able to confirm his suspicions.

It was a reasonable enough step for a badger, or a naturalist's best guess, from the wood to the bank. Perhaps the sett, wherever it was, had grown too small and a young boar or two or a nursery-seeking sow–whatever–had sallied out across the burn and found the brackeny bank and its old, cold hole, found its sandy soil easy to work, its south facing aspect more airily warm and conducive than the darkest woody depths. Or perhaps that was just me, unforgivably transferring my own thought processes on to badgers.

My listener mentioned another sett, just as long derelict, high on the foothills, in a corner of a forestry plantation, a mile away and across a main road, but what's a mile and a quiet road at night to a prospecting badger?

Later I put the information on to a map and found that first grain of truth at the heart of my rash hypothesis. There had been two setts in the osprey wood ten years ago, an occasional presence at least in the bracken bank, a sett in the foothills' forest clearing and who knows what kind of presence on the mountain beyond. So, with – as far as I knew – the exception of the mountain, all the landscape's stepping stones had held badgers, and their setts lay on the same north-south thread where my mind's eye had placed them. Now, I reasoned, if badgers were back in the bank, they were also drifting back into those other haunts up and down that old prime meridian between the wood and the mountain?

A few days later, after two badgerless nights out watching the bank hole, a phone call offered the advice that I could do worse than check out the old forestry sett in the foothills. I recruited my drinking cohort, who knew the place of old, and – crucially – the sympathetic farming family in the nearest house to the sett a mile up a hillside track. With their enthusiastic support, life for me, and for the badgers, would be much simpler. It was offered at once.

I chose a still May evening, too late to consider serious badger-watching but light enough to check out the sett and get a feel of the place. The end-of-the-track farmer had good news. There *were* badgers. He had seen them himself about six weeks ago. All he knew of for certain was that one of them came and went from an entrance which was clearly visible from below, where a 'couped-over beech' straddled an old dyke. He snorted his scepticism at the grapevine's suggestion that foresters had left the clearing unplanted in case the badgers did ever return.

'It was foresters who gassed the poor buggers in the first place,' he said, 'six years ago.'

The twenty-minute walk which followed became one of my spring-and-summer rituals. That two-mile return journey through forest rides would prove the last and longest haul and the most trying penance the conspiracy would devise. As if I hadn't paid enough in winter, here I would pay my dues in earnest. I would learn again what it takes to do this kind of kind of work. You put a routine down on the ground and you follow it tirelessly. Then, when you tire of it, you follow it doggedly. And when you can't face it again, you go out once more, and once more. It is that going again which I value above all the other tools of the nature writer's trade. I began to recognise my own trail as I pushed it through sodden grasses of that wet and wearying summer. I would learn the shape of my own footfall on grass. I would brush and curse my own path through eight-feet-tall bracken. I would cut my own profile into clouds of rain, mist and midges as I walked. And that first time of all was the only time I would walk it in company. My companion was a close friend of many years whose name would be enough to identify the place to too many people. So he must keep his anonymity so that the badgers can keep theirs.

We reached the sett at about 9 p.m. It was a rough rectangle sloping towards its south-west corner and more or less covered in bracken. The sett was in three tiers, or at least its entrance holes were, which is not at all the same thing, for the labyrinthine underground of it all was anybody's guess, only the badgers' certainty.

The topmost holes were in the very crown of the sett. I thought of that slope as a vast woodland whale, blowing badgers up into the night. Other holes, linked by horizontal paths, were dug into the slope in two level tiers a few feet apart. According to the farmer's recommendation and my friend's memory of a dozen years ago, we made for the fallen beech, but on the way we crossed the sett itself to make one close-quarters examination. From its dug-out doormats and meticulously clean entrances and fresh tracks and dung pits and a new groove over this spoil heap and that, we were as certain as we could be of badgers within. That would have done me for the night. Disturbance enough for any badger family, I thought. It was absurd to expect badgers to emerge with our scent so fresh on the sett. The experts said so. Tomorrow would be time enough. My friend said:

'I'm lucky with badgers, you know. We could give it half an hour. On the off chance.'

I shrugged agreement with no great optimism, for a badger is likely to put a lot of time between himself and two sets of wellies wiped on his doormats.

We waited anyway, and I noted at once how the loud rumble of the burn at our backs cloaked any small sound we might make. The wind was doing away west with our scent, just enough wind to keep the

year's first midges down to a thinly tolerable film of irritation. A
woodcock chuntered over. A roe doe slipped into the clearing and
tiptoed down through it, stopping often, finding our scent everywhere.
She stared hard at our shadowy stance too, for sight is in her repertoire
of defences and compensates for what the badger has that she hasn't –
fighting qualities unmatched by anything in the wild bar a man with a
gun or a posse of dogs – or both. She leaned her ears at us, but she
found only suspicions, and these are not usually enough to drive off a
roe. She stepped quietly away, nibbling continuously as she went.
Doubtless there would be a very new-born calf close by.

We had given it twenty of the thirty minutes and were still following the deer in the glasses, keeping only half an unexpectant eye on
the sett, when that half-eye caught movement. There. *There!* In the
top hole. *A face!*

It did not thrust out of the hole, but swithered just inside, then
withdrew. But I knew that face. Where had I seen it before, for I knew
that vaguely preoccupied air? I recognised that raised and questing nose
which looked as if its mind was only half on the job. I know that bear-
face! It's Pooh!

But the face had gone again. It had been no more than a blink in the
glasses as I refocussed them from the deer. The sett went bleak and
grave-still. What the hell were we doing following the roe? I grew
angry, blackly inconsolable for five minutes. I felt as if I had suddenly
abandoned my trust in nature when I should have relied on it utterly,
and I felt as if nature in its badger guise had withdrawn, betrayed. I was
still cursing myself when the same bear face pushed through a second
hole a few feet lower than the first. It pulled a badger body out behind it
and just stood there. He was a big boar badger and he was standing
there, thirty feet away in good daylight, and he was a bear.

He was the most bear I had ever seen, and still he just stood there, as
different from all the shadow-shrouds of all those interminable shivering winter darknesses as a cane from a corkscrew.

My first daylight badger resembled all my darkness badgers in one
respect only, the whiteness of his black-striped face. But no night-time
badger looked like this much bear, not small-eyed, preoccupied Pooh.

Then he was walking, side-on and huge, surprisingly long as he
reached out into his stride, so much bigger than all my shroud badgers,

so much more purposeful, solid, striding, so much more bear! He turned half towards us and I saw that nodding, swaying head. Then he crossed a dip in the ground and walked up out of it with his hind legs well below his forelegs, his head towards us but turned down so that the black stripes of his white face seemed to merge into the dark fur of his chest. He halted a stride and stopped with one foot raised, listening. I saw him for what he was, archetypal badger, and I thought him quite fine.

He nosed off into the grasses rustling noisily over cushions of dead bracken. Then he turned his back and his great grey hind quarters were the last we saw of him that night. He wasn't Pooh at all at this end, more Baloo, swaying slightly, pushing the grey flanks of him forward, propelling the bear face through the dusk until he was gone. A voice whispered:

'I told you: I'm lucky with badgers.'

He was always a compelling talker, especially on the subjects of foxes and badgers, for his life had known more than its share of both. He now ventured among his badger memoirs, years of them, and the listening was good, the grapevine coughing up rather more now than I had put into it. But I had contributed the first seed, and once the grapevine learned of our night's work there would be new eyes all along our allotted portion of the Highland Edge, scouring old haunts. If badgers really were beginning to drift back into the old places down threads of race memory, prospecting the twilit places of their forebears, they would find the Highland Edge more to their liking than it had been for many years. Times and attitudes do change, and half an hour in the company of such as the Pooh-faced one goes a long way to win new friends for badgers.

The conversation recalled earlier badger exploits, watching every night he said, and they would emerge five minutes after the first woodcock at 9.45 p.m.

'What? Every night?!'

This was the kind of generalisation which infuriated me, the hallmark of the badger specialist.

'Well, almost every night.'

'Even in winter?'

'Don't know about winter. You don't watch badgers in winter. No point.'

Oh, *that* kind of every night. I thought about my winter nights down at the Holly Glen and on the shore of the firth, and fumbling for the broken sink in the black wood, refusing to use the torch, and thought, one of us had got it wrong. Right then, I couldn't have said for certain which one of us.

The voice suddenly owned up:

'Funny about not finding a sett in the osprey wood, all this time. I'm sure they are still in there. But it was the same in a place we used to work in the south. We found tracks everywhere and hunted for them for months, and we never found them. Sometimes ... it just happens. Sometimes on their own ground they're better than us.'

A week later the phone rang again and a new voice hinted at a mountainside where a wood clings to a colossal upheaval of rock, a monumental steepness of grand frowning gestures, a hillside chequered tree-dark and bare-buttress-bright, south-facing and sun-smitten and wind-torn, and a toilsome plod on a hot day. Without asking whether or not I might know of the place, the grapevine voice advised that it had been rendered unmistakable in the winter when a high rockface had burst massively apart and one of the mighty fallen fragments now shone silvery in the sun. As I listened I put into my mind's eye the view north from the osprey bank with the badger hole, and I saw high above the foothill sett the rearing mountain face where the same high rock glittered where it had snagged and stuck fast.

'There were badgers in there twenty years ago,' the voice said, 'and if you're looking, I'd be interested to hear what you find.'

So from that single hole in the bank I had thrown out my fanciful badger threads invented through my own wishful thinking in response to a chance view of the Highland Edge from that Lothian shore. Now I had substantiated the whole thing as a historical fact. As I replaced the phone, I wondered at the nature of this conspiracy which in my mind at least had attended every hour of my badger endeavours. Now it seemed to have contrived the less than credible coincidence by which I had returned to the landscape of the Highland Edge looking for badgers which I had been told were not there, only to find that they had chosen this of all seasons to come curiously home from their exile, wherever.

6

All in the Mind

'GET THERE BEFORE SUNSET.' The words occur in precisely that order so often, and in so many different contexts where advice is proferred on the subject of badger-watching. You treat it as the first commandment, if only because everyone else does. So you get there before sunset, or if the sun hasn't shone for a fortnight you look up the time it's supposed to set, and agonise about whether the badgers know what sunset is. In hill country does it just mean when the sun slips behind the hill, or when it dips below sea level which no hill badger ever saw? But say the sun has shone and you can see it dip and the land yellows and you say to yourself, 'Now', and you pack your watch and your torch and your camera and whatever else you need to watch. Perhaps you need none of these things and you derive all you need from being still and watching, in which case you and the badgers you watch are the lucky ones.

There will be a point in your journey where you step beyond the reach of the sun, probably into trees, and the sun that made a bright open page of the fields beyond the trees now only dapples. Your eyes tone down the glimpsed other world through the leaves and adjust to the woody realm of badgers.

Well before the rest of the landscape has pronounced 'sunset', you lose not just the sight of sunlight but also the sense of it. The sun is of the sky and the broad places. The badger is of the ground, the grass-and-bracken tunnels, and the underground; his preferred direction is down. The badger wood darkens while the world beyond only pales. Nowhere grows darker than the woodland floor where you must discern movement.

At the hillside sett in its clearing, the only other option to standing in the lee of the couped-over beech or sitting astride or side-saddle on its trunk is a wispy willow I immediately christened 'Willow-the-wisp' and greeted it daily as such. A kink in its trunk six feet off the ground offers an excruciatingly uncomfortable seat or a tremulous stance while peering down into the sett's blowholes. You choose standing or sitting on this undernourished woodland runt according to your physical stature. Say, for the sake of the argument, you sit, and having sat and settled and stilled, you have put in place the first act in the small ritualised theatre of the badger watch, or at least of the badger watch as I have come to know it. This routine is a far better reason for 'getting there before sunset' than anything the badgers might have in mind.

The extreme discomfort of the seat, for instance, persists for no longer than three-quarters of an hour. During this time you probably fidget, or, if your upper lip is stiffer than mine, your eyes and your mind will fidget, and the quality of the watching is imperfect. Eventually a kind of benevolent numbness begins to mitigate the discomfort and your powers of concentration hone and intensify and focus more critically.

It will occur to you suddenly (and it will take you by surprise every time) that you have been silent and quite still for some time, and the intense heart of the watch has begun. Discomfort is now meaningless, and because it no longer matters it plays no part in the crux of the vigil. Nerve ends unite in a bond of common purpose, senses grow warier and you see deeper and think more lucidly. A ladybird couldn't cross that dark floor without activating the trip wires of your awareness. It is for this reason that you should get there before sunset so that (if he is coming out at all) the badger emerges during the intense heart of the watch, not the fidgety overture or the dull-eyed epilogue.

There is a point, too, in all end-of-the-day observations of nature when the regime of nature changes. You do not see it change like the Palace Guard, but if the quality of the watching is good enough, you will become aware that it has happened. Regardless of calm or storm, heat or cold, or whether your subject is a badger or a wintering goose horde, you sense that something has grown shallow and withdrawn and something has advanced and deepened. They are not easy to put a name to, but they are the forces of day and night, and they are the laws by which nature regulates the landscape. You may never be able to name them, but if you are exposed to their shifts often enough you grow sensitive to them. When the quality of the watching is good enough, you change with them and your own night forces deepen and advance. I am least happy as an observer of nature going out into the pre-dawn darkness for that very reason. The hour denies the opportunity of acclimatising to the forces of the night which have grown unnatural to mankind. Stepping from your house or your car straight into the darkened landscape is a hopeless cause and you startle at every sound. But if you have worked quiet and contemplative through the first owl hour you smile and put names to the sudden sounds.

The badger emerges, you watch, and if you watch well, a gaggle of badgers can swarm about your perch and not know you are there. When they disperse to go about their business in the same mood of secure wildness as that in which they emerged, you have done your part well.

It is then that you sense another change and you expel your pent-up tensions. It has grown difficult to keep your awareness at the same intense pitch. You climb down from the tree and remember the pain again. You are no longer a fragment of the badger wood but a fish out of water. As you pull out from the near darkness of the wood you find the world beyond a staggeringly pale place, the sky emptied of clouds, the fields pale fawn and wide and bright and startling, whereas when you crossed them to enter the wood they were just fields. If your sett lies on the Highland Edge of midsummer, it will always be daylight of a kind when you leave. You pause and look back at the field edge towards the sett, and suddenly it is the confined space of the sett in its dark woodland which is the fish out of water, the exception to the landscape rule. It is always good to be out in the openness of the place again, breathing easily and widening your focus with your horizons. That is why it will always be a taxing study when you go in search of badgers.

If, in the process of going and going and going again and again and again, you can improve the quality of the going and the watching; if you can learn a little badger-ness (and a little is all you will ever learn supposing you go every night for a lifetime), and come not only to question their ways but also to wonder at them, you can pay a badger no higher compliment.

★

All through that spring and summer and on into earliest autumn, I trekked up and down from the osprey wood to the mountain and back. In that diversity of landscape, and in the Lothian woods about the cottage (where I kept half an eye open between writing and forays north-westward to the Highland Edge) was all the variety that a novice badger-watcher could wish for. I was painfully aware that I was seeing far fewer badgers than the veterans who chose a single sett, put a seat up a tree and sat there. But I wanted just this diversity, I wanted the badger in his elements, not just the woodland dark of the sett but out on his range and on as many different ranges as I could track down. I also wanted to work in landscapes which meant something to me. The Highland Edge had accounted for almost half my life's wanderings, and the Holly Glen in its niche over the hill from the cottage, bright with reflected river light even on the darkest night and soothed with curlewsong four seasons of the year, was a doorstep gem I did not want to give up completely.

Yet it was the mountain which promised most, and even as I was planning a day-long reconnaissance the grapevine came up with its final offering – confirmation of two badgers briefly glimpsed at 1,500 feet in that precarious wooded boulderfield.

I got to the mountain before sunset and climbed through light rain which thickened at intervals into downpours. It is a mercifully brief climb, for it is no ordinary mountain.

'Well, it would be, wouldn't it?' I told a grapeviner later.

'Why?'

'Why? Because they're badgers.'

'Meaning...?'

'Look, you know more about badgers than I do. All these years in the field, you know very well what I mean...'

'No. What?'

It was said with such finality, and the incomprehension was so complete that I was quite taken aback. How could this badger-watcher be unaware of it after decades yet I, with less than a fragmented year to my credit, had been captivated by it almost from the first. I asked for descriptions of all badger landscapes in my companion's repertoire. They went back a long way and covered an impressive geography, but every one was a summer sett in deciduous woodland, and mostly,

63

I was told, you could set your watch by what a badger did and when, to which I said:

'Bullshit. This,' I said, 'is the cunningest, cleverest, choosiest, canniest beast I was ever privileged to rub shoulders with. He is foxier than foxes and...'

'Hah!'

The grapeviner was even more fox-watcher than badger-watcher. He had raised foxes, revered them, loved them for their foxiness, and now gave a short eulogy that put them king of this wild realm to a badger's court jester. I listened, then said:

'You see in the tod what you miss in the brock, because you never stepped beyond the shade of the sett. You missed the individual, the decisive thinker, the discretionary retreater, the valorous warrior, the opportunist, the tactician, the imaginative...'

'What's imaginative in a badger? Enslaved to the same paths day after day, night after night, year after year ... that hardly shows imagination, or choosiness, does it? Stupidity, yes!'

I could hardly believe this now, that one could watch so much and see so little. I said:

'How can you be enslaved to paths when you are yourself the architect and the engineer and the maintenance squad of the paths? Every path has its purpose, purpose arrived at by decision, and as for choice, why has that wee sett on the hill got nine holes for four badgers, and paths thick on the ground as spider legs on a spider?'

'And why have there been no badgers on the mountain for twenty odd years?'

'Because they were probably gassed or driven out, just like on the hill and in the old sett in the wood.'

'Ah, but only once, not twenty times, once a year. They practised discretion and judged it not safe for twenty years. What brought them back? Why now? Because they sensed the climate was better, the mountain safer, the Highland Edge safer. Look at the evidence we're gathering of them returning all over the Highland Edge. They drifted back because of their own judgment, and they have found their judgment sound.'

'You're not serious,' said the grapeviner. 'Where's your evidence for *that*?'

Young osprey grounded and (right) an old nest in the osprey wood

Roe deer calf, about one week old

Boar emerging from its hole on the Highland Edge

'I was amazed to see a family of two turn into a family of four!'

'It's out there in the wood,' I told the fox lover.

'The wood? We still don't know for sure there are any badgers in the wood.'

'Not the badgers,' I said. 'The ospreys.'

'Eh?!'

'It's the same thing ... the forgiveness of nature. Nature in its osprey guise was driven out, right out of the country. But nature also held the race memory intact, and when the climate changed and things were easier for the hook-beaks, the ospreys began to drift back in. It was forty and more years, mind, but what's that in the lifetime of the species? Now look at our ospreys. What is it, a hundred pairs? And thousands of people driving hundreds of miles to queue up and watch them. The climate changing, the judgment of nature.

'Now, all along here, where so many people – you included if you remember – said there were no badgers, here they are from the wood to the bank to the clearing on the hill to the mountain. It's still tenuous and it may falter or fail, like the ospreys did at first, but here it is. It's the badger that's made the decision to come back. *That's* being choosy. It was also cunning and canny, because look how carefully it's been done. They were well set in the hill clearing before anyone knew about it. And if I hadn't had this half-daft idea for my book, who knows when we might have tumbled to them up on the mountain?'

The grapeviner shrugged and shook an exasperated head as if to say, 'I teach you all I know and you give me this stuff back.'

I made my excuses and left the bar, for I had only an hour if I was to be on the mountain before sunset.

7

No Ordinary Mountain

HOW HAD THE GRAPEVINE ever found this place? I felt particularly grateful for that crucial assistance which pointed me here. Without it I might have taken months to find what was the most secretive sett I had ever seen. But the race memory of nature is in folk too and some of the memories on the grapevine are as long as the osprey's.

I had stepped from the open hill into a green mountain labyrinth. I realised at once why the wood has survived while elsewhere the mountain boasts no higher branch than a stag's antler. It survives because it cloaks a 1,000-feet treachery of boulders, a colossal landscape tumbledown. In the clefts and crevices between them a tree can lodge and root and prosper and create its own damp shade where other trees can gather and grow. In such nervy places a sheep or a deer goes warily if it goes at all, and never in the kind of hordes which nibble forests to the floor.

Any contour line you choose across the mountainside smirks from the backs of boulders or the depths of some abyss, gleefully watching your underfoot discomfort as you step up from a mossy bog and slip back knee deep from a sodden and splintered toehold.

The most jungly aspect of all this relents suddenly into a small and almost level clearing a few yards wide. To the north the mountain rears immensely. To the west a gap in the trees shows mountains leaning ever closer. The south of the clearing is bounded by a stockade of small trees, hazel mostly, with whippy trunks and rooted on a rock shelf which ends abruptly in a small crag. I skirted the edge of the shelf, rounding one more hazel a little more robust than the rest, and a small ramp of bare earth and flat rock trembles, down to the foot of the crag where two

66

rocks had collided aeons ago and fused over the centuries into a rough right angle. It is a chaotic little place of uncertain footings on slabby rock among ferns and skinny trees. Where the rocks meet is a small dark hole at ground level, an innocuous and barely visible hole to the casual eye. If you are studying every foot of the ground as you go, you will find the ramp suddenly spattered with a thin litter of earth and leaves and branches. It is, in this unearthiest of places, what passes for a badger spoil-heap, and the freshness of it suggests that the badger is at home.

There are two possibilities: watch the hole from in front where a flat rock with twiggy birches sprouting from it offers a stance twenty yards back, or from a nearer boulder, lower than the hole and garnished with a wide cap of moss and tall feathery ferns. The latter is a daring vantage point to try once I get the feel of the place, but it is possible to watch from behind and above. Two trees flank the clearing on either side, both climbable and more or less tolerably uncomfortable, but neither with a view of the emerging badger, although there were enough hallmarks in the clearing's grass and mosses to suggest that a badger might linger there.

I chose the back rock first, the most discreet option. As I stilled by the birchy screen the midges found me and established at once a new definition of what is and what is not tolerable in terms of badger-watching. As long as the rain confined itself to lacy sprays the midges clung in thick clouds, and only laid off during the downpours. And as I suffered the alternating deluges of rain and midges and studied the dark rock-and-tree mountain world through its thick grey light, I wondered by what yardstick a badger under ten feet of rock might judge that sunset had come and gone.

My rock was the last outpost of a mountain shelf. Bracken was broken up by small boulders and one vast gently-sloping flattish and monstrous rock, a whaleback warm with moss and lichen and scratched by the tracks of badger claws. The trees, a good native mix of rowan and oak as well as the flimsier birch and hazel, shut out the wider mountain world and exerted a quiet tension on the place. They also kept out much of the mountain wind. No midge could dream of a more conducive arena in which to ply its bloodthirsty trade. At my back, one more precipice spilled away down the mountainside to taller trees and fewer rocks, but ahead, and high above the hazel waifs, lay the greatest chaos of broken rock. A soaring, roughly-tiered wall led up to a patch of sky the width of a small house and loudly crossed by a troubled peregrine falcon.

A woodcock was cruising the showers, and if there would be one residence trickier to track down on the mountain than the badger's it would be the woodcock's, chameleon bird that it is, still as a fallen branch on the woodland floor when it sits tight. Far across the glen at my back a cuckoo was wearing down a two-syllable groove on the evening and owls were mobilising. In the long, long June night light the trees all around me still thrummed and hissed and whistled with the diligent to-ing-and-fro-ing of small birds – tits mostly, but warblers too and a black-bird, and blurring wrens. Being badger country, a robin perched on a twig not three feet from the hole and poured out song, that song which (so my pet theory runs) falls on every badger ear the length and breadth of the land.

The song cut out suddenly. The small whirring tick of robin alarm replaced it, and the twig was robinless. He had sensed, seconds before I saw, the vivid white shape moving deep inside the rock. From the distance of my stance the badger entrance was nothing more than a small dark shape, not a dug entrance like a woodland sett, but a space where two boulders lean together. The white, swithering badger face now showed just how deep the entrance ran. It seemed to my eye to travel a long way forward before it emerged into full daylight, restlessly questing for a snatch of the mountain wind. And when, inevitably, it withdrew again, it reversed so far back into the mountainside that I saw it dim before it vanished.

When it returned, it thrust much faster out on to the gloomy shelf of rock which forms a ramp down to the hole before ending in a cul-de-sac against a rock wall. The badger, a smaller, slenderer beast than the boar on the hillside to the south, paused full length on the ramp, turned the slim skull of a female towards me, saw and sensed nothing untoward in the thickened shadows of the birch-and-rain screen and moved leisurely along the ramp, swivelled sharply upwards on to the shelf of the clearing and was at once lost to view.

Now, I told myself. Now. Catch hold of this moment and hold on to it. Look at the line of that sleek stretching badger shape as she climbs the rock from the ramp to the clearing! The mountain badger is a rock climber. Watch the shape of it change, not bear nor Clydesdale but (what she *really* is, biologically) weasel, a huge, lithe weasel that mountaineers for a living.

This is the badger you fancied in your mind's eye from the high fields behind the cottage above the Forth. This is the climactic moment of the trail you drew on a map – that trail which began darkly by the broken sink in the black wood. This is the highest endeavour of the grapevine and the conspiracy, which now seemed to have welded into a single benevolent force. You have worked no harder for anything you've won in nature than this.

I stood in the gloom and the rain and the midges while the cuckoo havered on and on, mercifully distant, and the owls soothed the passage of evening into darkless night. I dripped, itched, sweated, but I felt as though nature had suddenly stepped up on to the rock beside me, unlocked a door I was incapable of opening, and whispered:

'Look. While you're here, have a look at this.'

So I looked and worked at remembering, and my reward for the care I took with the moment is the memory – indelible and new-minted even now – of the door in the heart of the mountain, of the badger which crossed its rock threshold to answer nature's summons.

More than anywhere else I had encountered, except perhaps in fields behind my cottage where the Holly Glen's small woodland wedge gathered, I could latch on to the sense of a badger realm here on the mountain. It is, I have felt from the first, too limiting to think of the badger solely as a woodland animal. It is like thinking of the osprey as a tree-top bird, because that is where it happens to nest. The badger lives out that part of his life which is an organised society in the wood but he goes beyond the wood for his living. Once he has slipped the leash of the sett's conventions and constraints, he becomes that freewheeling and imaginative individualist which I have come to admire so much. He makes the acquaintance in the process with fellow travellers of which the sett-watcher is largely ignorant and which his woodland image denies. On the high fields, for example, he supplements his earthworm preferences by scooping a day-old leveret from the form while the hefty doe thuds spatulate hind feet into his flanks, then runs swiftly beyond the reach of his snarling retaliation.

Up here on the mountain, he is as familiar with the anxious screech of a peregrine falcon as with robin song. The far-carrying sound-scythe of buzzards will reach his ear even in his deepest, coolest, furthest-back chamber. I wonder just how far back his chambers go here. How much does he actually excavate in this rockiest of realms, and how much is just a linking of hollows fashioned by the haphazard fall of one rock on another? He will know too that wild heart-stopper common to every mountain-thirled mammal and bird, the momentary darkening of eagle shadows. It is not that the eagle would consider a healthy adult badger as prey – too much like hard work and no certainty of winning the argument should the badger uncharacteristically choose the valour of combat rather than discretion. But the golden eagle's overlordship is acknowledged by all nature on the mountain, or at least as much of it as is watchful enough to feel threatened by that unmistakable shadow's fall across its path – and that will include the recolonising badger.

Most likely, if he has drifted in from lowland strongholds, as I suspect, he has never seen eagles before, but his race-memory has, and just as race-memory impelled him back to the mountain, so it will have equipped him through instinct or reasoning powers or both with a good fear of eagles. Likewise, the mountain's eagles may well have never seen a badger, but would know what to expect, and know to avoid the possibilities. All badgers will step aside from men and eagles unless circumstance denies that option, in which case man or eagle will know they have been in a terrible fight. I had heard of all this in the past, for it is part of the imbibed lore of the wilds, and from many first-hand accounts, it is a justifiable reputation. I have now added credibility to that reputation by watching the muscular bear-packaging of badgers at close enough quarters to be impressed.

So now my badger endeavours had evolved geographically from the broken sink of the black wood to this high point of exploration, seeking out badgers among eagle shadows as I set out to climb the mountain.

The climbing would serve three purposes. The first was to examine the sett in detail in daylight and check the sticks I had laid across the entrance late the previous night. The second was to watch the mountain through a long day, learning the landscape of the badger's world and its fellow travellers on the mountain. Although I knew something of the mountain of old, I had never climbed this mountainside before, nor gone about the place in a badgery frame of mind. It is a good way to go, for by homing in on that single, low-slung, ground-level facet of the mountain, you pull the rest of it into a new perspective: you look *at* the mountain you climb, rather than at the view from it.

The third purpose of the climbing was the self-indulgence of stretching my own definition of a badger realm a contour or two beyond what was strictly necessary, to push up through the airlessness of wood and bouldery bracken, up into the airy treelessness of the high crags where the peregrines split their patch of sky and a black gully spilled a sudden cataract of ravens. And yes, I would be forever watching my path for eagle shadows, my sky for the shadow-thrower.

All this reflected my determination to put the badger in his widest context. How much more even this cloistery mountainside sett would mean if I climbed *down* into it in the dusk after the long mountain day, rather than clutching at the same old straw of a few evening hours after a day at the desk. I had got nature into a rut once through badger-watching; I would not let it happen again.

I stepped from the small road into the wood and found the morning mountain vivid and vital and zesty with small bird song-and-dance, and young buzzards wheezily fretful in their eyrie tree, a green claw on a low crag. The deeper green of the badger's slice of the woodland was like entering a maze, shutting out the wider, higher mountain at once. My mind's preoccupation became the next green yard. Would that foothold hold? Would that boulder stay still? Would that yard of foot-wide footpath lead to another navigable yard or a cul-de-sac terminating in a small abyss or a black crag? I reached the sett, found the sticks pushed down in a way which suggested an animal going in, and allowed myself a small satisfied smile at that.

How different the place looked in the morning light. How good it was to be able to move freely through the small arena of that mountain shelf, as easily as a badger, parting its green curtains, crossing its maze of waist-deep rocks and brackens to the grey wall of its backdrop where the main entrance nestled at the end of its dark ramp. There was, I now discovered, a second entrance I had not seen before, half hidden by tall elegant ferns (a quite different proposition from wretched bracken), smaller than the main entrance but swept clean as any regularly used badger threshold. It was also uncomfortably close to where my feet would be if I used the forward rock as photographic hide, as I had hoped to do. A little carelessness with an eddying wind or an ill-considered movement and I could spend a very long time looking at a blank wall. There was also the comic prospect of a badger tiptoeing out of the lower hole behind my back while I frowned in frenzies of concentration at the main entrance.

I sat for a while by the ramp, looking down from a small rock shelf at the debris cleared away from the entrance by the badgers – twigs mostly, scraps of leaves, and a little loose soil. Compared to the earthworks of lowland woodland setts it was nothing at all, hardly worth the digging and sweeping. I thrust my mind deep inside the skin of the mountain. I have never got used to being at a badger sett during the day, knowing that there is orderly life going on under my feet, most likely aware of the human presence above but secure and at ease with it inside that black and blinded underworld. It is arguable that no sett could be more secure than this. There would be no 'terrier boys' to worry about. Too arduous a climb, too far back to the car with their hideously won prize, and the kind of terrain which you could only dig into with dynamite – and with a fair chance of bringing much of the rest of the mountainside down on top of you in the process.

It is trickier terrain for badger-watchers too. There are none of the clear-cut trails of a lowland sett, those badger highways and byways through woodland and copse and field and under fences and over dykes and fallen trees which lead you surely through the animals' night world. On the mountain there are only hints of paths, a few brackeny yards, then rocks and holes intervene. There is no way of knowing where a path leads from such a spot. Are those scratches on the rock's mossy garb the spoor of the badger where it jumped from the end of the path and clung on for a footing? Or do they mark the fall of a sharp twiggy branch thrown down in a gale? Or do they denote the hurrying passage of the hill fox through what he well knows is a patch of the mountainside which has been reclaimed by badgers? Or are there (as I suspect, as yet an un-confirmed suspicion) wildcats up here? If there are wildcats in this neck of the mountain woods, what do they make of the badgers, and vice versa?

So you clutch at straws when you go trailing uphill from the sett entrance, and before you have travelled far there is no discernible trail at all and more straws than you know what to do with.

There were also more holes uphill, but old and overgrown and badger-cold. Each hole had its barely discernible yard or two of path, and there was a twofold hole, two entrances, one above the other, and leading to the same burrow. That small discovery made me wonder about another adaptation dictated by the terrain. All the holes, all seven of them, lay in more or less the same narrow swathe of hillside, but it was a vertical swathe, and this, I had just realised, was a vertical sett with much of the communication between its chambers conducted above ground. I had also begun to wonder about just how permanent or otherwise this new occupancy of the sett might be. Only two holes out of seven were being used, and these two were the lowest on the mountainside and very close together. There were none of the hall-marks of a family group. The grapevine had suggested two badgers, so possibly an unconsummated pair of young adults were looking for a patch of their own. They would only stay if they liked what they found. There seemed no reason why they should not stay, except perhaps the presence every few days of the same distasteful human scent, my scent. But then I also believe that wildlife as sophisticated as a badger is capable of distinguishing a benevolent presence from a malevolent one, and of learning to tolerate the one as surely as it reviles the other. Or is that, I asked myself in the same moment as the idea occurred to me, wishful thinking and self-justification? Anyway, I was here, and so were the badgers, and for all the fleeting nature of our encounters, neither of us felt disposed to pull out. Yet.

A hundred feet above the sett, the woodland began to thin. The trees were more stunted and erratic, and often rooted improbably in the rock itself. In such places, a rowan or a birch needs precious little encouragement. It will prosper modestly if left to its own devices – in this case, if it is not browsed to the bone by sheep and deer. As the trees thin, so the rock thickens, and gathers its self-importance immensely into ever more impressive formations.

You climb steeply now towards a fractured wall which partly obscures greater walls, far back and far above. You squeeze through a gap and at once you are locked into a hidden mountain world of heaped statuesque rock. Stone in all its forms is here, a rough grey amphitheatrical wonderland. You try to grasp the transition: moments ago you were on the other side of its containing wall, suspecting little, the sun bright on your back and the mountain falling away beneath you in ever-deepening shades of the woodland's green; the next (following a thin trail which *could* be a badger path), you pushed between two rocks and suddenly the ground fell before you a few brackeny feet. You stood here, shut in and astounded. The rock crazy-paves the floor of this airy mountain chamber with gargantuan cobblestones. It stutters round a rim to a fat craggy pinnacle. It culminates in a deep grey head-wall where even the summer-ripe sun can strike no shade of mitigating colour. It is a dour wall. Yet the whole mass of the chamber was patched with vivid green and yellow grasses and flowers, modest tufts of yellow saxifrage and plump cushions of alpine lady's mantle, and here and there among all this the pointedly outrageous purples of orchids. Purple! *Here!* Nature works these tricks sometimes, a scene-shifting so sudden and so overdone that your eye struggles to take it in and opts instead for a pin-prick of purple.

I crossed the floor of the amphitheatre, looking round and taking in only the aura of the place, not its substance. Soon I was homing in again on one more (the most outrageous) purple flower, a flourishing plume of an orchid extravagantly perched on a high and overhung ledge above a small rock chimney in the mountain wall. It looked so exotic, and the climb so much fun that I forgot for the moment that I was supposed to be travelling in badger mode. With my back against one wall and my feet against the other, I shouldered and pushed my way up to the ledge, marvelled at the fertility of the place, drooled over the orchid's small magnificence in that mighty rock landscape, and was about to climb down again when a small sunlit ramp above my head snapped into focus. What made it remarkable was the fact that it bore no relation to the rock mass I climbed but seemed to float beyond it. I climbed on, intrigued, and emerged above a hole in the mountain. It was a long, narrow and curving hole like a grotesquely overdone slit-trench. I stood on its shady side, the ramp on its sunny side, and between us, twenty feet of thin cool air.

Realisation moves slowly in such circumstances, like a stalking wildcat, then it leaps and the reality of what you confront is a sharp squeal of something like pain. Somewhere in the mountain's story, the whole mass of the amphitheatre, several acres of it and unguessable thousands of tons of rock, had slipped, had moved away from the embrace of its parent mountain, and was now attached only by its floor. Now it sat out on its own shelf like a monstrous raven's nest on a crag the size of the mountain.

I scrambled back down past the orchid ledge and found a perch from which to watch the whole rock chaos and its tottering walls and its green and cobblestone floor. Did the badgers ever come up here? Although it might have been on a different planet, it was no more than half a mile from the sett, the going nothing more than steep, the ground lush in patches and easier to work, if anything, than the wretched floorlessness of the sett area itself. Here a badger might well encounter eagle shadows and look up beyond the range of its reliable vision and comprehend at once the meaning of the great winged shape, and if circumstances permit, shy instinctively away. For the moment, however, the birdlife was disappointingly prosaic. No cries more dignified than the squabble of jackdaws ricocheted like bullets off the rocks, echoing among the crags.

What a place! To think I had climbed this mountain more than once and not known of its hidden tremulous offspring. And even if I had yet to prove, or even convince myself, that badgers came here, it was because of the badgers that I had found it now.

I whiled away an afternoon hour there over a late lunch, still and silent enough to take advantage of the unlikeliest prospect that a badger, day-nesting somewhere on the hill, might come exploring. But nothing moved below and only the jackdaws moved above.

I had packed and stood to go when I sensed rather than saw movement far down on the floor among the largest of the cobblestone-boulders. I snatched for the glasses and hit the eyepieces against my chin. When at last I united eyepieces and eyes, there was nothing to be seen.

What *had* I spotted? I cross-examined my mind's eye but could pin down no clear image, nothing more than that I had detected animal movement at that furthest corner of the rock amphitheatre near the gap by which I had entered. I worked the glasses hard across the bouldery landscape, but it yielded nothing. I knew what I was looking for, of course, even if I did not know what I had seen. The naturalist in me lodged a protest at this point, trying to play down the surge of excitement I felt, for I was already concocting badger imagery with a quite unwarranted certainty. The naturalist wanted proof, visible evidence. I wanted badgers. I had been thinking badgers all morning, I had taken badgers in my mind up a mountainside which is not something I had ever done before in all the mountainsides of my life. I had mused on badgers over lunch and suddenly there was movement among the rocks, and it was badger movement. I would have put my life savings on it at that moment, admittedly not a considerable sum, but I would have put it anyway.

If I had done so, I would have been instantly bankrupt and the naturalist in me utterly vindicated. As I dropped down through the rocks towards that far corner, making what haste and care I could, the very clear shape of a red fox leaped from the midst of the boulders, paused on the broken wall in mocking clarity and with its characteristic lithe and agile spring, vanished on to the open hill beyond.

Stealth abandoned, I followed at speed, a giddily exhilarating boulder-hopping sprint, the kind of mountain movement you can get away with once in a while in a frame of mind of euphoric confidence. I surged across ground where two hours before I had picked my way with badgery care. Now I was leaping the boulder tops where before I had threaded a path between them. I reached the wall, almost danced up it, and hugged its rampart with only my eyes clear of its shadow. The fox was not a hundred yards away, prodding the base of a rock with his nose, a big beautiful and bronzed dog fox. He was on to me at once with his better-than-badger eyes, and as he ran up the bracken slope he leaped again and again like a working dog to see where he was going above the bracken, and where he had been, and whether I was following.

8

A High Old Time

H E WAS THE BIGGEST red fox I had ever seen. He was thickset and
long, and as he leaped clear of the bracken for a sighting of the
danger from which he fled, his tail bannered out behind him, thick as a
windsock and as long as his body. When he ran in shadow he was tawny
and taut, but when he leaped up the sun was full on him and he shone
and flew unfettered.

I leaned into the lee of a big rock twice my height and put the glasses
on him. Abruptly he sat. He had run enough from this foe who would
not give chase. So he sat to see what stillness and watchfulness would
achieve. I kept my own stillness and watchfulness, and for timeless
moments we were the oldest protagonists on the mountain, hunter and
hunted, but the hunted was hunter too. I spoke words to him he
wouldn't hear, but perhaps he would catch their drift. I told him I was
watcher, not hunter, and harmless to him, and admirer not adversary.

So I watched him watching me, a disembodied fox head, the torso
and brush of him sunk bracken-deep. Occasionally he craned his neck as
if he were uncertain where I was, or perhaps willing some movement
or sound out of me to confirm I still stood in my shadow. His gaze did
not waver, not until a raven coughed and he looked up, unerringly
pinpointing the sound. I thought of how often I had looked up on a
hundred other mountainsides in search of the same sound, and spent
whole minutes looking too high, too low, too east, too something-
or-other, before the right bird would appear in the correct sightline.
We look – most of us – with less than fox eyes, something we have
in common with badgers.

The fox face returned to its careful study of my rock-shadowed
stillness, but he permitted distractions to temper vigilance, my threat

diminishing in his eyes. Once I saw him snap at a white butterfly as it flounced past, so close that his head barely moved. The butterfly did not emerge from beyond the far side of the fox. It was a poor year for butterflies anyway. The fox rose and began to walk slowly uphill, pausing often, curving his whole body round to look directly back at me rather than looking straight back down his spine, which is the roe deer way. Then he broke into a purposeful trot along a new climbing diagonal, a course aimed at a specific and obviously well-known vantage point. He was approaching a deer fence, but he made no attempt to run alongside it looking for weaknesses. Instead he made straight for a tall gate of perhaps a dozen or fifteen horizontal bars. From two or three feet back he jumped at this barrier and seemed to hit it running. He continued running, vertically, paused memorably with all four feet on the top of the gate and the tail straight out and still, then he scrabbled straight down the other side. When he hit the ground he was already back in the same measured trotting gait. It was all done with a kind of studied nonchalance born of a much practised routine.

Soon, out on the wilder hill beyond the fence, the fox's attitude changed utterly. He became not a purposeful trotter but a meandering explorer. What he was doing, of course, was hunting, but he was also mountaineering in the sense of climbing a mountain and deriving a form of satisfaction from the act of climbing. He would contour for fifty yards, perhaps a hundred, then cut up a mazy diagonal, but at every excuse and sometimes without one he would pause, scent, mark, scrape, prod. He would stop often to look round, occasionally back down towards me, my intrusion not forgotten but no longer preoccupying. Mostly, when he stopped to look round, it was to look far out over his mountain realm.

I had been working hard at the watching, the glasses rarely off him in fifteen minutes, and lowered only briefly to keep a sense of him in his wider landscape. Slowly I gained a sense of what was going on up there. Here was an animal not just working for its living but relishing the moment, the mountain, the hunt, the climb. He was in his perfect element, strong and limber and imperious, fleet and fluent. And I was as sure as I could ever be without trespassing among the thought-paths of the fox mind that he was *enjoying* himself. For all the lethal nature of his climb as far as small lives of the mountain (beetle, bug, vole, bird) were concerned, the fox moved with leisured ease. He was not just quartering the mountain, he was also exploring it. He would scramble up a steeply sloping buttress and pose on its crown when the hunter might have done better to comb the shadowy gully or the deep heathery flanks. Then with the sun full on him, burnished as any autumn stag, he turned through 180 degrees and presented his other profile. There was, it seemed, no purpose to the pose other than the pleasure of being fox and stepping out on to an airy mountain pedestal and surveying from its unique perspective his habitat in its rarest and most benign mood. No mountaineer will need to be convinced of the intense and rarefied nature of such a pleasure. It was news to me that a fox should think of it, gazing out at horizons in a way that, I imagine, a badger never would.

The fox was on the move again, and this time I moved with him. I took a parallel diagonal to his, and I stopped when I saw him stop and curve and look back and down. I waved to him and he stared. Then, having doubtless convinced himself that my plodding pace was no match for his fastest four-legged potential, he ambled off uncaring of me, inspecting new gullies, drinking beneath a waterfall, clambering up the rocks by the very edge of the white water rather than the easier slopes outwith the burn's gully. He was still enjoying himself.

I lowered the glasses to negotiate a rock step of my own, and when I raised them again it was to find a foxless hillside. It was not hard to see where he had gone even from two hundred feet below. A pair of wheatears had begun to yo-yo up and down the air just above the nearest skyline, chittering frantically. Clearly the fox was much too close to a nest for their peace of mind, and when he re-emerged on the skyline, following his nose into a jumble of boulders, the birds were flying within inches of his head. He had snapped at and caught the butterfly (a piece of play as far as the fox was concerned for sure from the jaunty manner in which it was done) but he treated the demented birds and their circles as though they were not there. Then he was among the rocks and the muzzle of him went in deep. It came up again chomping, and the wheatears' futile limited repertoire of abuse became nothing more than a frenzied dirge. The thing was done and the fox climbed on.

I lost him over the next mountain rise, but I hurried up to the wheatear cairn to see if there was any evidence of slaughter. There was none. Not a vestige. Had I not been fox-watching and had I happened on the place five minutes later I would have had no inkling of what had just been acted out here. I would probably have put the new rage of the adult wheatears down to an over-zealous streak of protectiveness, possibly caused by the exposed nature of their home territory, and given them as wide a berth as the crossing of their boulderfield permitted.

The fox was high when I found him again, the explorations seemingly as whimsical and haphazard, crossing faces, threading up gullies, circumnavigating crags, contouring and climbing, always climbing, presumably towards the limit of his loosely defined territory. On such a day of sunlit summer ease, what was there to hurry for? Let's have a high old time on this high old mountainside. At about 2,000 feet, and having followed the fox's uphill doings for about an hour, I began to wonder how high I was and how much time I had. Badgering had long since been given up. 'I can always badger down,' I excused myself. Besides fox and badger were fellow travellers on the mountain.

By now the raven's nest was below me, and being the earliest of the mountain's nesters, the brood were flying strongly, the nest in decay. But somewhere further up and further back was the peregrine's crag. It would be unlikely, I thought, that the fox would be as indifferent to a mobbing peregrine overhead as to a wheatear. I toiled after the fox, sometimes losing him, the distance slowly widening between us, but always able to pick him up in the glasses again where he skylined on the steepening ground. He was a hundred feet higher when he took another brood of wheatears. They were almost fledged this time, and mobile enough to scatter among the rocks. I saw first the parent birds at his head again, then I saw him prance like an alsatian pup and, in that attitude of skipping play, snuff out three tiny lives. Again he treated the adults as if they did not exist.

I have often wondered about that moment. Was the peregrines' attention attracted by the small shrieks of the wheatears watching from inches away the fox devour their offspring? Perhaps, however, the falcons had been watching the fox anyway, and utterly indifferent to the dire plight of the wheatears, had decided to dissuade him out of their territory. The problem with being a wheatear is that your shriek of protest is simply too feeble. A peregrine, on the other hand ... now there is a shrieker for you. I well remember the warden on St Kilda leap from his seat at his cottage doorstep when that uniquely piercing yapping yelp drifted down from the sea-cliff eyrie of the island's peregrines, a mile away and almost a thousand feet higher.

At the first syllable on the badger mountain the fox head was up and so was mine. (I too have been mobbed by peregrines and I didn't like it.) The shrieker was the female. She was already close before the fox noticed her. The falling shadow from several hundred feet higher was the tiercel, headlong as a dropped stone. He flattened out and cruised in a few feet above his mate and added his voice. The fox's response was decisive and instant. He ran. He cut one more diagonal uphill, but aimed well away from the peregrine crag. Did he *know* the liberty he was taking so near the falcon territory and retreat along a predetermined course? The way he now climbed was quite different from his every other movement on the mountain. He kept to the short mountain grasses, avoided the boulders, and put swift distance between himself and the disturbance. The peregrines dropped their guard and vanished. I watched him run and cross a last skyline – too high for me to have a chance of catching up with him. As he ran I came as close as I ever will to knowing what it must have looked like to watch a wild wolf cross a Highland hillside. A curious thrill touched me at the thought, and stayed long after the fox had crossed the skyline and gone.

Scotland has been wolfless now for 250 years. Its extermination was a cause for celebration in the Highlands of the 1740s, even if there was nothing else much to celebrate. There are several claimants to the title of the slayer of the last wolf, but the most celebrated was that of a stalker called Macqueen. The beast in question had supposedly killed two children in the north-east Highlands. Macqueen's account is almost as famous as his deed:

> As I came through the slochk [pass] by east the hill there, I foregathered wi' the beast. My long dog there turned him. I buckled wi' him, and dirkit him, and syne whuttled his craig, and brought awa his countenance for fear he should come alive again, for they are precarious creatures.

So the child-slayer wolf was suddenly grown docile enough to permit the stalker to wrestle it, dirk it, cut its throat and permit itself to be beheaded. But such was the all-too-believable unremorse at the fact of the wolf's extermination that man has never quite forgiven himself. For the last forty or so of our 250 wolfless years naturalists have pricked that conscience into consideration of reintroducing wolves. The idea has grown respectable enough for Scottish Natural Heritage to give it tentative voice. The most likely consequence is an initial experiment on the Hebridean island of Rum which the SNH owns, and where it is involved in a long-term study of the Highland wolf's favourite prey, the red deer. It is a promising proposition for nature. There is widespread agreement that the Highlands hold far too many deer, and in a confined island environment with a good mix of Highland habitats it would be relatively simple to study the impact of a controlled number of wolves as a natural predator on the deer herd.

We have learned to live without wolves, even if we have not learned to live with the deed which exterminated them. Somehow, in our moribund and bureaucratically top-heavy era of conservation, room must be made for wildness, a gesture towards nature purely for its own sake, serving only the cause of wildness. The wolf's resurrection would be such a gesture. It was once the head of the food chain of the wild Highlands, the golden eagle of the mammal world. If Rum proves to be a beginning rather than an end in itself, the wolf might reign again, and the questing fox and the foraging badger on the Highland Edge will find a new and troubling scent on the night wind.

9

Badgers of the Broken Mountain

S OMETHING SHONE. It shone in a way I once saw a new and unrusted corrugated iron roof shine on a Shetland croft. But it was no tin roof that shone. It was the mountain which shone, and the reason for the shining was that it had burst apart. We tend to look upon mountains as symbols for permanence in the transience of our lives, and certainly the stillness and the quietude I encounter among mountains are the breath of life to me – no – the breath of a greater life-force, to me. But mountains move. They shift, they spill, they shrink, they react under the pressure of nature's irresistible forces. And here, last winter, a fifty-feet tapering rock buttress 2,000 feet up the mountain burst apart.

A week after the fox encounter, I climbed again up that great mountainous tumbledown of rock and rock-wedged woodland below and above the badger sett with the idea of examining the mountain's high and shining light, and descending to the sett before sunset. The buttress looked permanent enough from far below, its familiar triangular front as old and impenetrably grey as ever. From closer the cracks appear, cracks as wide as your hand, then cracks that would take your shoulders without you touching the sides, and from every dark artery of that fractured rockface there spring a dozen diagonal offshoots, veins of new frailty. Then, once you get clear of the trees, the shining wound appears. For it was a wound which shone.

A wedge of rock had fallen out of the buttress and smashed on to the mountainside below, on to the rocks of a previous calamity in the mountain's story. None of it has travelled far, but its smithereens have formed a new treacherous boulderfield on the shelf below the butt-ress. Cross it and every other rock moves under you, a millimetre or a foot, or it falls over on itself and throws you into unbalanced collisions with its neighbours. You stand again, bruised and grazed and bleeding from two fingertips. At one side of the boulderfield stands a wide and tall dish of rock, the biggest intact block from the fallen wedge. Its west-turned face is as open as a sattelite dish. It used to be locked into the inside of the rock buttress, but now it stares out the evening sun. It is that which shines, glittering as tinfoil, bright as a corrugated roof. It is, in its raw and wounded way, beautiful. It stands where it has wedged, on edge, but there is nothing permanent about where it stands. You do not have to be a geologist to guess with a fair expectation of being right that this is not its last resting place.

The buttress, too, is not done with the mountain-moving. The cracks show where other pieces are ready to fall, ready to add to the treacheries of the new boulderfield, waiting. They wait until the relentless downward drag of their own weight hauls them out of the ancient bond, the time-shrouded (but not timeless, not even mountains are timeless) embrace of the parent rock. Five hundred feet below – directly below – in the precise path of the landslide, should it ever come to that, is the badger sett. Perhaps it is not as secure a proposition as I had imagined.

Does the badger know all this?

Was he here when the mountain moved?

Did he hear its explosion, feel its foundation-trembling in his own rock lair?

If he heard and felt, did he know its meaning?

If he knew its meaning, did he climb to reassess the wisdom of his new surroundings?

The last is the least likely hypothesis, although it is hardly credible that he would be unaware of the state of the mountain. Most likely is that he knows the mountain has moved, but he lives for the day. It has not moved this far down, not yet, so it is not relevant. And however fluent is his race memory (which after all has tucked him quietly back into this mountainside) the idea behind the phrase 'not yet' is not in his repertoire of ideas. There is either event, or non-event. There are no anticipated events.

The mountain was deeply shadowed when I left, although the broken rock still shone, albeit with a fainter, more muted shining.

'Get there before sunset,' a voice intoned in my dawdling head, and I saw that the sun had gone from the hillside across the glen. The pink light of an hour ago had withdrawn uphill like a rolled blind, and now the hill was grey-green and softened and stilled. I realised I had spent too long too high for the safe arrival at the badger sett. I began to think about badger timetables as I set off downhill. The earliest I had seen them emerge here at this time of year was shortly after 9 p.m. and now it was nearer 10 p.m. I considered an early night, but opted instead for a fast descent and a careful hour above the sett, just in case. I hurtled down as much of the slope as I dared and only let stealth intrude in the last 100 feet downhill. I came on the small flattish clearing above the sett rocks, the 'roof' of the sett itself, putting every footstep down slowly with good discretion. Now, stop, yards back from the sett. Test the wind. Listen.

Sounds on the air. Grunts.

Groans, then yelps, snorts.

Grunts again.

What the. . .?

Freeze. *Listen*. Listen harder.

There are two clear voices. One loud, gruff, but further down the ramp (a guess, I can still see none of it). One softer, less aggressive, but nearer, as if it might be on the very nearest hidden corner of the ramp. Some of the sounds are quite unfamiliar to my ears, but I know enough of what I hear to recognise the vocabulary of badger. There are two badgers on the ramp that lies below the edge of the rock on which I stand. Four strides to the edge. Take three then drop on hands and knees. Crawl the fourth.

First stride: good, silent, balanced. Second: also good, heart-in-mouth. Third . . . a yelp from below, a scatter of feet, a badger on the rock face under my feet. How?

There is a second ramp, almost vertical, more of a wide crack. I had never noticed it before. Well, yes, I had, but never contemplated its role as a badger thoroughfare – too awkward, too sheer, too tight a turn out of the sett.

The badger and I meet head on at eight feet, I in mid-stride, he as his head pushes up above the level of the rock on which I stand. He dives down and sideways and what was (to my eyes) unyielding rock unaccountably yields. The crack is at once badgerless. Below, there is a blurred grey back (the second badger), and a smaller, sharp and upturned face, ghost-white, black-banded, then a vanishing scut. Then silence.

It is not wise, I think, to loiter round the sett, having gatecrashed badger intimacies. But then I am operating neither on the basis of conventional badger-watching wisdom nor, I believe, with conventional badgers. I am also captivated by the disappearing trick, and the rock which yielded. I claw down the rock crack the badger clawed up, and now I see his imprint in its thin earth and I wonder how I missed it. Halfway up its right-hand wall there is a wedge of space. It looks deep enough to take my arm up to my shoulder, but I wisely resist the temptation. It has, after all, just accommodated a startled, now acutely defensive badger, a big boar badger. The slighter one on the ramp below is presumably female. That fitted with the two voices and where they seemed to be coming from.

I visualise that muscular stretched bear-shape of the boar again. I look at the hole which is nothing more than a space between two rocks lodged one on top of the other and fixed there by nothing more than the growth of mountain greenery. That a badger should vanish there, without sight or sound or scent! It did not look like a sett entrance, not halfway up a six-feet rock wall, yet it was obviously a known strategic element of the badger landscape, unerringly sought out, unhesitatingly negotiated. The moment reinforces my belief that there is little scope on this mountainside for a dug sett. In fact the more I saw of these mountain badgers, and the more I heard from the grapevine, the less they seemed to conform to all the received wisdom which characterises woodland setts. There are no dug burrows, but they seem to live in just that kind of chamber, rock walled, rock floored, rock roofed, between blocks of the massive mountain debris. There are no reliable paths by which to plot their course, and they appear to be the least routine-conscious of animals. In the past month for example, mid-May to Mid-June, their emergence times – far from being reliable enough to set your watch by – varied from 9 p.m. to almost midnight. Twice nothing emerged at all. In the faltering light I saw the slender female coming uphill through the densest tangle of rock and tree, and going *in*.

What now? Pull out, give the badgers a breathing space, a day or two to recover? But, I argued with myself, I don't know that the badgers need a breathing space to recover. Maybe their only need right now is to be outside, above ground, and maybe the only qualifying factor is that they want to be satisfied that the danger which sent them helter-skeltering for shelter has passed. They were, after all, above ground when I arrived unforgivably after sunset. Perhaps all they have in mind now is getting back above ground again with all possible haste. If that is the case, then I know that beneath my feet are two badgers, that it is past their preferred time for emerging but still within the later limit of their range of emergence times, that if I can be inconspicuous and silent and still and stay close, I might reap an unexpected benefit because I got there *after* sunset.

Wind direction precluded watching from in front of the hole. That left two trees above the hole for viable vantage points, or . . .

There was a flat rock I could walk straight on to, and almost immediately above the sett entrance, that rock which made the ramp a cul-de-sac. I could lie there, with only the top of my head visible, and only visible if the emerging badger looked vertically upwards and behind when it was clear of the hole. I would be only six feet away at that point. If I lay still enough, I would be practically invisible. If, however, the badger came straight up the crack where we had just met head-on and happened to double back at the top, he would find my face two or three feet from his own, and at more or less the same level. It was risky, and adherents to the manual would be horrified. All that I would suffer if it failed was disappointment, and my badger year was already well accustomed to that. But if it worked, I would have learned a little more about badger tolerances. I might even learn something of their route out on to the mountain. Planning to watch them mountaineer was impossible, such was the terrain and so difficult the prospect of quiet pursuit, but a start might be made now, on the flat rock.

I reached my rock without a false sound. As I settled face down on its spongy mattress of yellow-green moss I discovered that it is on just such a mattress of moss that midges congregate when they are not airborne. Midges in unthinkable numbers now rose into my face, my nose, eyes, ears, hair, and penetrated every nook and niche in the fabric of my mountain jacket as if it were made of trawler net mesh. No chemical preparation known to man can counter such dedicated mass adversity. The solutions are either to watch your badgers in east coast lowland woodlands or light a bonfire and sit on top of it. It sounds funny. In truth, it is insufferable.

87

I squirmed, scratched, swore under my breath (a quite futile exercise at any time since a silent oath neither offends nor does it relieve the swearer of its vehemence, and what other reasons can there be for swearing?). I hauled my jacket over my head, cut the forward aperture of the hood to an eyeslit, and resigned the rest of my body to every imaginable and unimaginable form of midge-inflicted indignity. Inconspicuous, silent, still ... my writhings must have sounded like a thunderstorm on the roof to waiting wondering badger ears below. I prepared to suffer the insufferable for as long as it took. I inched forward to the rock's edge and peered over. It was the perfect viewpoint for the ramp, if unnervingly close to any emerging badger, but I hardly expected the sight which met my eyes.

The ramp is shielded by its fringe of hazel trunks close enough together to form a single canopy of foliage. There are six trees, each of many slim trunks, and all in a single rock-rooted row. The effect is curiously like a short, low tunnel, the trees and leafy branches forming one wall and the curve of a roof, the bare rock of the mountain forming the other wall. The ramp is the floor of the tunnel.

Seconds later and I would have missed the slim badger head turning into the tunnel from the far end, its body curving up and round the furthest hazel, then straightening into the tunnel. As far as I could tell it was the same female badger which I had startled into the main sett entrance when the boar had disappeared into his rock. Somehow, in the time it had taken me to soft-shoe a dozen yards and smother myself in midges, the smaller sow had found her way down the mountainside via the main entrance, presumably emerging at the one lower hole which was kept clear and in something like regular use. Then, for reasons best known to herself, she had climbed back up to the ramp where she now walked, apparently unconcerned, filling my head with questions. In fact, filling my head with questions is what badgers do best. I could make no sense of this ruse – beyond the unlikely chance that it was a third badger which just happened by at the crucial moment. No, I was as certain as I could be that the small and sleek-prowed blur with the upturned face I glimpsed below the boar was the same one which now approached me and stopped. And now sat.

I was beginning to find individuality's quirks in different badgers a reward of a kind for never having treated them as a species but as the most individualistic of creatures. This one sat back and contrived to look as if she were moving forward, her forefeet firmly planted and at ease but one in front of the other, as if she had been frozen in mid-stride. Then she lifted and stretched up a cluster of hazels, sniffed at and snatched a slug, dropped to the same walking-sitting pose and suddenly caught my eyes on the rock and froze. With malicious timing nature conspired a salvo of midges inside my hood and my reflex response galvanised the badger into a single fast turn and deft head-first descent off the ramp, making for the lower hole. Effectively she just squeezed through the hazels and dived down like an otter or a seal into the concealing ferns and brackens and rocks between the ramp and the lower hole. Immediately I realised that that was what she had done the first time I had startled her. She had not vanished into the main entrance, but as soon as she was out of my sight, she had negotiated the five-foot drop from the ramp and vanished beneath it. She had not gone underground at all! Suddenly my theory that there was little if any dugout sett here was on a sounder footing.

Now I had startled the badgers twice in as many minutes. Firmly convinced that that was that for the night, I rose gratefully from my midge horde. They fell from me in the grey rain like the drops of shed water a dog shakes off after a swim. I stepped down from the mountain hot and bothered, sore and itchy, and a bit mesmerised too.

There are sporadic accounts of badgers that accustom themselves to unlikely aspects of human presence. Few things on television have left me with a more uncomfortable feeling than the sight of badgers being lured into a suburban living room to feed on a carpet and (wisely) ignoring a lit television screen. What I have never seen explained is whether the phenomenon is true of badgers in wild landscapes where the presence of people is either rare and fleeting or non-existent. It was at times like this, confronted by what I considered extraordinary behaviour and being baffled by it that I acknowledged my raw inexperience in the company of badgers. I wondered then how the very first badger-watchers had come to their conclusions. Surely, with no precedents and only their own wits to rely on, they would take one scrap of observation, link it to a thought, and link the end of the thought to another scrap, and by trial and error and the fashioning of weak lines and strong, construct a true chain of thought. I now cast a link of my own.

I considered the small badger, so much smaller than the boar, perhaps a very young animal, one not accustomed to humans at all, perhaps fearless of them. At that, my own small chain of thought began to link itself together.

I had so little to go on other than eye and instinct, yet surely only a badger completely uncomprehending of a human being as a source of danger would behave so recklessly? I had assumed both badgers were incomers from the lowland side of the Highland Edge, but if the small badger was as young as I thought she was – perhaps a yearling – she was no incomer. I knew just about enough of the theory of badger family society to conclude with some justification that a year-old animal would still be attached to and protected by the family group. Even if this was the sole survivor of a destroyed sett (an unlikely coincidence), a lone journey to the mountain from the lowlands in her first year bordered on fantasy. She had to be a mountain badger. A mountain badger born and bred. I told myself aloud:

'She is still relying on her mate, the boar, and her race memory for her fear of man, because she hasn't seen enough of him to fear. Her first run for cover was sparked by the boar's impressive dodge. She didn't know I was there until she was already running! And she hardly fled for dear life, did she?'

She had been back, presumably looking for the boar where he had left her, in less than two minutes, and the way she came carefree down the ramp suggested the hoovering cubs I had photographed down at the hillside wood.

Yet if she was so young, that was no mate with whom she had been caterwauling. That was . . . a big brother! And if that was a brother, and this (another early suspicion) not a permanently occupied sett, then there was another sett in the glen, perhaps even on the mountain, near enough at any rate for its youngsters to tramp up here in a day's march, or a night's. It would explain the erratic timekeeping, the high percentage of blank nights, the small number of entrances in use. And if there was a main sett elsewhere on the mountain it was furtive enough to have eluded the grapevine, possibly for several years!

I was back on the mountain the next night, dutifully before sunset. Aided by a change in wind direction, I was determined to try the front rock, not ten feet from the main entrance and more or less at eye level. I wanted to see if either of the badgers would emerge with me so close. If possible I wanted to photograph them on that ramp, that mountain ledge which was the most impressive piece of badger sett landscape I had encountered. At the same time I was worried. It was not the badgers which troubled me but the rock, for it wore the same shade of mosses which harboured the midge legions on the flat rock above the sett. Well doused in anti-midge gel (a contradiction in terms – the only effective midge deterrent I know of is a forest fire) and with my jacket over my head and swathed in a waterproof suit and wellingtons – all this on a warm June night – I thought I could stand it for an hour. After that I would retreat up the edge of the ramp to an airier perch in a tree. I gritted my teeth and went in.

I had a small mat for the worst of it and leaned my arms flat on that; the rest of me lay on the steep slope of the rock. Fully stretched, I could just touch the ground with my boots. Thus almost all my weight was on my tiptoes. In this position, defenceless against the midge, I intended to hold a camera more or less still for more or less an hour. The combination of mat, hooded waterproof jacket, and the extra light jacket thrown over my head (a camouflaging shade of summer green, I hoped) kept the worst of the midges from my face but not from the one bare hand which held the camera, nor from the camera itself.

Stillness is not really an option in such circumstances, but the reward was an unobscured sightline right into the hole. If I could be still enough, and more important, quiet enough in my midge-fending movements, who knows? Photography was never a crucial part of the project, but a handful of good pictures showing the badger in his landscape were certainly desirable. Here I wanted the animal away from the entrance and padding up the ramp ... eight feet away if things worked out the way I wanted them. I tried a couple of one-handed test focussings, but found the viewfinder image an incomprehensible blur. This was resolved by using my pinkie to turn the most compact body of midges I have ever seen into a mass grave. More movement, of course, more oaths, futilely silent of course. It is one of the drawbacks of badger watching that you cannot curse out loud, for it is a singularly curse-inducing occupation.

A shadow moved deep inside the hole. The numbing pain in my feet vanished at once. The shadow hardened to a Hallowe'en mask, then to a badger face. This point, this coalescing of the features of a badger face still inside the hole but lit by the wan daylight of midsummer evenings, this is the perfect compromise, the ideal way to re-define your badger between the flashlight image and the shadow-shroud of the black winter wood. He only comes out in summer daylight, of course, because in Scotland there is not enough darkness in which to hunt safely. For a few seconds, the badger face was perfectly poised, engagingly lit, intriguingly disembodied.

The face rose to the hole, wavered, tilted snout revolving slowly like a great telescope casting across the sky. The wind was being tested, sifted, shredded for clues. The head and shoulders and one forefoot crossed the threshold and stopped. It was the big boar. I saw him push up on his hidden foot and the bulk of him massed behind his head and moved out on to the ramp, but he was dissatisfied and turned and went in again. I breathed out, let my head fall on to my camera hand, hardly noticing an eyeful of midges. This is the time at which you can blink and miss the thing for which you have suffered. Pay attention. I was scolding myself. It wasn't done yet, and I knew it wasn't.

The hardening shadow was back again in three minutes. He came without a pause, straight from his stygian stronghold into unnerving daylight, turned from his threshold on to the ramp and turned at once again, straight up the rockface where yesterday we had met head-on. I had set myself and the camera for a photograph on the ramp, so I had to move to snatch a hastily recomposed shot, and at the sound and the flash he was twisting sideways back into the unyielding rock wall which yielded, and I have a bad picture of a rock.

I have a good image too of the badger as a supple and undulating curve. From the moment he emerged, from his first forward stride out of the hole and up his yard of path to the ramp, he began to curve back in towards the rock he had just left. He began to curve because he was already clear in his mind that he was going to use not the ramp but the wide crack up to his rooftop. So he curved as he emerged and he began to climb as he curved. There was the single four-footed stride forward which took him clear of the hole, then the forefeet took to the rock at his back and he curved into his short climb. When the flash fired he snapped the curve into a tight twist, and unless I miss my guess drastically, he would be back in his sett's deepest recess in seconds.

What impressed me was the taut control, the elongation of the bear body into weasel suppleness, the power of the pushing feet, the poise of the climbing. In human mountaineering, the great climbers are the ones with perfect balance. I fancy I was watching a great climber among badgers, and I instantly regretted firing the camera for a photograph that had a poor chance of being a good one. It both cut short the climbing and betrayed my presence when, by holding still and waiting a little longer, other opportunities might have been offered.

I had waited enough in such conditions, and having created the disturbance anyway, I took the opportunity to vacate the forward rock, and take to the tree above the sett. The sudden near-absence of midges and the breath of mountain breeze was like the splash of ice-cold beer on a parched throat. I sighed a mighty gratitude. At least I now knew that the front rock was a watching option, albeit a hostile summer environment. Perhaps in September . . .

It is rare to be comfortable up a tree, especially a small tree with spindly branches and sharply angled forks, but I was breathing freely and I had the weight off my feet and a light wind in my hair. This was living again!

After I had been still for five minutes, I had a family of newly fledged blue tits for company. They fluttered into the tree with the clumsiness of bobbing corks, and when they perched they looked as if they had stepped out of the worst kind of over-cute birthday card. Their perfectly formed blue tit feather pattern in muted colours was topped and bottomed by uncontrollable comic twists of thistle-down feathers, the smallest feathers imaginable, barely visible, but just visible enough to look really silly. The birds came within three or four feet of me, calling continually in fast triplets and semi-quavers, their shapes blurred by the soft edges of the thistledown, curious rather than fearful of the strange dark growth in their tree. Then they were gone, fluttering and semi-quavering through the wood. I had the tree and the mountain wind to myself once more, and suddenly the mountain felt vacant.

I looked around at the mountainside and its woodland and bracken, at the glint of loch far below and wedges of other mountainsides up and down the glen, at the rocks beneath me where the badgers had holed up, at my own preposterous position seven or eight feet up a tree.

Suddenly nothing seemed to fit. I saw nature not as a single mono-crystalline unity but a thing of unco-ordinated fighting splinters, every splinter consumed with its own tiny survival. All jarred, from the blood-lusting midge and the useless slug through the infant blue tits to the tentative badgers, the fox, the wheatears, the thrusting show-piece orchid, the high fliers – raven, peregrine, eagle – suddenly I could see no balance to the thing, no sense of purpose in any of it. Hadn't the very mountainside just demonstrated by its winter wounds how it was nothing more than a loose amalgam of splinters?

Then in the midst of all that bickering and biting and blood-letting and breaking apart there was the most absurd splinter of all – me. My presence on the mountain was not only excruciatingly uncomfortable, it was suddenly pointless. The more so when a clutch of blue tits of all frail and flighty things could waft their humdrum unconcern before my eyes. Here I was, wedged up a tree, attempting to be as unhumanlike as my species permitted, another splinter prickling against its habitat. I was also attempting – futile fool! – to stake my claim to a closer walk with nature, preaching harmony and understanding to as many people as could be persuaded to pick up one of my books or a newspaper piece or a poem, while all the time I was racked by a sense of discord and incomprehension, mauled by midges, snubbed by badgers, and dis-missed by blue tits not yet old enough to feed themselves.

It was an unnerving hour, one of the drabbest I have ever spent. Its mood was like an acid eroding all the things I believed in, everything on which I had staked my writer's life. The ghost of the black badger wood of the broken sink had resurfaced and was prowling round the base of the tree, throwing blue tits at me. Or was it just one more capricious twist of the conspiracy just when I had begun to convince myself that it had had my interests at heart all along?

The crisis passed as suddenly as it arrived, but it left me with a numbing legacy that was not improved by the appearance of the female badger. She had come up the ramp, picked up my scent there and followed it all the way to the base of my tree. Then, without looking up, or looking any further, she had turned her back and stalked off into the bracken, swaying slightly, rustling the undergrowth as she went. I climbed down after that and sulked downhill to the car and the long drive home, where I rebuked myself and determined on the only possible course of action. The next night, I would go again.

I was at the front rock by eight. I saw no badgers at all, but a buzzard cruised over as I climbed and hung briefly over my head, then swung away to answer the summons of her young on a nearby cliff. And while I was crouched by the rock with my back to the sky, an old familiar screeching fell on my ears, the mobbing alarm of the peregrine falcon. I looked cautiously round and up, and there he was, ripping open his patch of sky in short anxious sprints. Then the buzzard hove into view and the peregrine sallied swiftly off to engage him, and while they spun and sprinted through their aimless dogfight they screeched and wailed, and I felt myself slip my hand back into nature's glove because the falcon had treated me the same way as it had treated the buzzard. The ghost of the broken sink was banished.

10

A Crowning Sense of Purpose

THE HILLSIDE is the Highland Edge, the Highland Boundary Fault of geologists' vocabulary, though to my eye it has been for the most part a faultless place. The hillside lies in three folds above the osprey loch, the lower slopes either wooded by nature or forested by man, and farmed in a small way. My badger forays up on to the mountain were sporadic ventures beyond the Highland Edge, but it was here, between the osprey wood and the hillside sett that I wore down my man-trail through spring and summer and gratefully into autumn. If the mountain was the badger realm at its most rarefied and the woods of Lothian the workaday polar opposite, the hillside forest is the workable compromise. It holds hints of Highland and Lowland Scotland but it is primarily defined by a distinctive landscape presence of its own. It has always felt more Highland than Lowland to me (although that is probably because I almost invariably approach it from the south) but it is a softer subtler place than the full-blooded Highlands and I was never anything other than comfortable there.

The ospreys had begun again in a new tree, five giant firs to the south-west from the one which had served them well for ten years. Why change now only they will ever know. The new tree tapered to a blunt crown and they built directly on to that, so that the eyrie became the treetop, and in its last-of-the-light silhouette it looked like a volcano crater. It was a strange paradox: for almost twenty years I had been drawn here by the ospreys which inhabited the attic storey of the woodland. Now I lurched in my mind between that exalted height and the badgers in the basement.

On 19 May, two days after a brief heatwave had the female osprey panting on her eyrie through the noon and afternoon, it snowed. I sat

The view from the mountain woodland

The mountain rockfall above the badger sett

The lower entrance to the three-tier mountain sett

Boar badger emerging from a rock crevice

A badger's claw marks on a fallen tree

A Highland Edge cub begins to find its feet, watched by an attentive mother

Mountain badgers have to be practised rock-climbers

on the bracken bank beyond the osprey wood in the lee of a sheltering thickness of whin bushes watching this tawdry winter lout of a storm impose its dark out-of-step regime on spring's finest hour. The bank was blue, a heady smother of wild hyacinths, fringed with the canary yellow of the whins, masses of them which trailed down the flanks of the bank like a carelessly worn scarf. By the badger hole, the solitary hawthorn was unfurling its first brilliant white blossom. In the grey-white deluge which the mountains had flung down on the loch, and the loch and its wide-open winds now hurtled east across the wood, all that splendour was so much squandered show, nature's mannequins shrivelling and bedraggling in their finery before my eyes.

I put the glasses on the eyrie for a reassuring glimpse of the bird on her eggs, fearing that if the nonsense persisted she might desert. It had happened to golden eagles that wretched spring, all across the Highlands. I stared hard, which in my own nature-watching vocabulary is a euphemism for not seeing what I wanted to see. But I kept staring because from time to time the sleety-snow curtains parted for long enough to unblur the forest and I needed to catch such a parting and peer through it. At last the eyrie tree, sodden and lightly whitened, revealed for ten seconds the dark wedge of an osprey tail protruding above the rim of the nest crater. It was all the bird that was visible, but it was all I needed to see.

Working on the ill wind principle, I considered the possibilities of turning the same snow to my advantage, an aid to tracking the badgers up the hill – or wherever – from the woodland sett. I was still new to the hillside sett, but already behind me were that first daylight encounter and my first detailed exploration of the sett which suggested cubs in residence (flattened bare patches around the sett entrances) and a partiality among the adults for the open heather hill above the plantation forest (distinct paths heading off in that direction from the sett). If the snow held until evening, there might be just enough on the hill to show me the badger way up. It was a forlorn enough hope because snow at this time of year is a fickle and a fleeting creature. I could do worse than be at the sett early and wait and watch. So I drove the five-minute mile of a four-gated track, left the car at the farm and squelched off into the forest.

The snow had stopped, but its wind still sliced lumps out of the hill

Mountain badgers have to be practised rock-climbers

air. Spring is a sluggard up here compared to the osprey wood 300 feet below. It sounds too slight a difference, but there is none of the bank's brilliance here and the solitary hawthorn in the midst of the sett is still unblooming.

I walked quietly along my chosen trail through the rides and out into the top of the sett's clearing in the corner of the wood and hard by the burn. The wind was not right, but I trusted to its steady blast and the lee of the fallen beech and the burn's big trees not to let any scent linger about the holes. It's the fickle meandering breezes which are the problem. Besides, I was well below the holes. So, crouching in the beech's shadows and darkened by the burn's trees, I waited. The snow had left barely a footprint's depth lying in the forest, so wet had it been, but here and there among the tatters of shredding cloud on the hill there were glimpses of whitened heather slopes and small screes. It needs to stay cold, I told myself, and the badgers need to be out early, and they need to go straight uphill. The chances of this kind of May snow telling me anything were very small indeed.

In the next hour the sky lightened, the wind fell and I watched the white drain from the hill almost by the minute while the clearing stayed badgerless. By 9 p.m. the sky was brighter than it had been all day and the midges were out. A thrush began to sing somewhere behind me. Suddenly the whole hillside had acquired a monumental stillness and the sound of the thrush flowed up and out unstoppably over the clearing and hung there like a silver cloud.

Out into that stillness came the boar. There was the same precautionary face at the higher entrance (from this lowly crouch by the beech it looked like nothing so much as a face at an upstairs window), the same thoughtful withdrawal, the same unhesitating emergence from the lower hole and the left turn which took him down the hillside and away from the slopes where the snow had briefly lain. The snow no longer mattered. It had been a motive to spur me up on to the hillside when otherwise I might have lingered on the low ground. It had served its purpose and now I had the boar badger in my glasses and the unstemmed flow of thrushsong in my ears. In the stillness the badger was as audible as he was visible while crossing the clearing. He made for a corner of tall grasses where there were several dung pits, vanished discreetly there, but was soon thrusting among the grasses again, pushing up towards the back of the sett where he would cross my man-trail. I was curious to see what this unflappable boar might make of my trail, even though it was now two hours old. If I could follow him up to where our paths would cross, and if he set out to pursue my trail, I could follow him following me . . .

I stepped out from the beech and followed him. The thrush sang and sang. Nothing else moved but the badger and I and the burn and the stream of pure silver song.

The boar stayed about fifty yards ahead, but his every movement showed in the grasses and he crackled the underfoot matting of last year's bracken. The thickness of the matting worried me, and the tall, tightly furled fronds of the new growth suggested that watching the sett could become very difficult indeed once the bracken was at its densest. It is a plant without a saving grace, although it does die exquisitely.

Suddenly the significance of what I was doing caught up with me. It was as if, stalking a badger along its own footpath through that Highland Edge spring night, I turned in response to someone tapping me on the shoulder. I turned and saw myself then in a manner which has occurred before but only in the most isolated or introverting of landscapes. I had a clear vision of myself from high above, so that I was an inch-high green jacket and that dark barely discernible wedge a fragment of the whole hill range ahead of me was the badger I was following. A year ago I had never watched a badger in the wild, nor for that matter had I felt inclined to do so. Now I was wholly wrapped up in this utterly indifferent patch of moving grass which occasionally bared a grey-black rear view of a shapeless bear. From high, high above, we were scraps of the hillside, pushing a path through sodden grasses across a tiny clearing in a corner of a small forest on a flank of low hills which spilled and dipped away in three directions towards the inevitability of the mountains. In all that, only the mountains would hold the tilting eagle-eye, for he would have dismissed the moving scraps of man and badger for what they were, but he would be troubled by the whiteness of the mountain. He would not hear, nor would he see the singing cloud of song thrush, and in that respect alone, my viewpoint was preferable to his.

The high vision snapped shut in my mind and my footfall on the grass was suddenly too loud in my ears. I stopped in case the badger had heard, but nothing had changed during those moments of day-dream. At the high-point of the clearing, another badger path radiates out from the top holes of the sett under the hawthorn to a junction with the perimeter path which the badger and I followed. As I reached the junction, so did a second badger. It was scarcely less hefty than the boar, slighter of face, and probably his mate. She stopped. I stopped. She sat back and stared. I stood and stared. We were perhaps ten, twelve feet apart. She snorted, turned and galloped. It was a bear gallop, it crashed across the clearing in marvellous bounds, as ungainly as it was formidable for the undisguised power behind the gait. Then silence, apart from the thrush.

What had happened to the boar? No grass moved.

I pushed my luck and strode purposefully up the path he had just made, saw the wet grasses he had bent and broken as he passed. There was nothing. If he was still in the top half of the clearing, he was not above ground.

Then I came to a second junction, less clear than the path we had followed, and there was the brush and broken grass. This was where, while his mate sounded the alarm of her retreat, he had glided soundlessly back to the sett and I had not seen him go. The thrush carolled on, louder in my ears now. I retraced my steps, contoured all the way round the clearing back to the couped-over beech and sat down again. Now what? For want of a clearer course of action, I waited without knowing now why I waited. Slowly I grew still again and settled into that deep phase of the watching when, as an observer of nature, all things are possible.

A single buzzard cry sliced through the cloud of thrushsong, a falling, elemental cadence, a thing woven out of thin air. The bird drifted, a compact dark male, down over the higher forest, moving sideways, led by the fingertips of one spread wing. In that attitude he crossed to the middle of the clearing and came to a standstill hovering on heavy wings. It was beautifully done. He held himself there, pinioned to the air, wings and tail flexing and fanning, body still, head down and working round every corner of the clearing. He looked long and hard at my shape but again and again he turned his head away to where something in the grass held his attention. He dropped lower, ten feet perhaps, and his yellow legs dangled briefly as he fell. A reflex action, I think. He was looking harder at whatever he was seeing. Then he cried again, and with the same sideways glide he was gone, far over the forest. As he left a small blunt shape whirred past my left shoulder and vanished into the hawthorn above the badger sett. The thrush, signing off after (I checked my watch) an hour-and-a-half of more or less unbroken song. He had stopped singing while I was riveted to the buzzard and I had not heard his last coda. The cloud of silver he had layered above the clearing dispersed, and in its place was a chill and a deeper quiet. From high and far off, a cuckoo called, and a robin flicked between the hawthorn and the willow, chittering softly.

I was still pondering what it might have been that the buzzard was so intent on when the roe doe ghosted down between willow and hawthorn, treading a badger path, stopping often, nervous, wary, silent. There was a movement at her feet and she bent low. A tiny calf stood to greet her. She licked its muzzle, its dappled flanks. It reached out to suckle, fed lustily, then stood beneath its mother, looking round at its new world. Was this what had held the buzzard's attention, eagle-sized prey rather than buzzard but intriguing enough, and so new-born that perhaps it looked briefly appetising?

The calf began to walk away, a tottering progress through undergrowth often taller than itself. The doe was feeding and raising her head often to watch, listen, scent the wind. The calf must learn quickly, must know where she is, must know where to lie still and where not to do so. She had reached a small slope twenty yards away from her mother. It was far enough, the doe took a step towards the calf and the young adventurer (perhaps in response to some muttered rebuke) made its best speed back to its mother's side. Together they wandered off up past the badger sett.

The badgers and the roe obviously know each other, and consider each other no threat. The boar could kill the new-born calf effortlessly and quickly, and in these first few days of the calf's life, its only defence in its mother's absences is stillness. How often in the next two or three weeks I would hear the doe's barked command, a sharp and deep contralto note, instructing the calf to lie low while she broke cover and drew attention to herself. I made a mental note to come early on my next visit and have a good look for the calf.

I turned my attention back to the sett. As hard as I watched it now, my mind and my eyes kept wandering. I was too tired, and the core of the watching had passed. I had decided to leave, and bent down to pick up my pack and stow away my camera and my glasses when my eyes came level with a bend in the horizontal trunk of the couped-over beech. It wore a pattern which seemed to cut across the lines of the bark, parallel and pale lines in threes and fours which began and ended abruptly, the hallmark of badger scratches. I had spent the evening by the badgers' scratching post, without realising it! I had seen badger scratched trees before, and had assumed in my ignorance that it was a consequence of climbing, to catch slugs, for example. Now scratches on a fallen tree made no kind of sense, and rather than test the grapevine on anything so specific and subject my work to the scrutiny of more 'experts', I broke one of my own rules and consulted the best reference book for an answer to a question. *The Natural History of Badgers* by Ernest Neal rose mightily in my estimation by conceding an unexplained mystery. Dr Neal writes:

> ... When a badger uses such a tree, it gets up on its hind legs, reaches as high as it can with its front paws and then brings them down, scraping them against the bark as it does so ... This action has been described as claw sharpening, but that is clearly incorrect, as no such action will sharpen the claws; rather the contrary.
>
> It is not at all certain why badgers do this ...

He goes on to suggest explanations – one, that it tones up muscles after sleeping the way many an animal stretches when it wakes, but he inclines towards the idea that it helps to free mud from between the toes after foraging, citing the presence of mud on many a scratched tree. But all that is applied to growing trees with rough bark. My couped-over beech had no bark left on it. The trunk was perfectly smooth, but it had clearly been scratched many times over many years. I liked Neal's third try:

> Another possible explanation is that a scratching tree serves as a visual or scent signal which would have a territorial significance. It is known that the wolverine, which is a near relative, marks trees near its den, but this appears to be due to repeated chewing and biting. Consequently, the trees become very conspicuous and may function

as visual signals. Unlike the wolverine, badgers are mainly nocturnal so a scratching tree is unlikely to act as a visual signal for them [possibly less true this far north where badgers are out in good daylight for a third of the year – May to August], but it may well act as a scent marker... You also find scratch marks on fallen tree trunks which indicate repeated rather than random use.

It is clear that more observations are needed before the full significance of these 'scratching' places is understood.

A wise and untypically open-minded expert is Dr Neal.

The roe doe was back in the clearing, on her own again having couched her calf, and relaxed enough not to have noticed me in the beech's shadow before I noticed her. She was feeding on the leaves of the willow, standing not more than a dozen yards from the top holes of the sett. She was also relaxed enough to suggest a state of mutual tolerance with the badgers. Not far off there would be a buck, and in his rutting prime he too is a formidable fighting foe, even for a badger. So the odds were more or less even, and they left each other alone, and got on together that way.

The woodcock was on the roding beat, croak-squeaking his Duke Ellington riff, and he dived down (the first time I have ever seen such a thing) and buzzed the roe deer's head where she stood. She looked more surprised than offended, and her head moved steadily, turning her gaze through 180 degrees until she stared right down her back, watching the flight of the woodcock and wondering why.

There was a movement in the sett, a scuffle in the grasses, a small squeal by one of the unseen holes – the cubs at play? I put down the glasses on the beech trunk where I sat, bent to pick up my camera and, as I straightened again, knocked the glasses to the ground with a thud which sounded in that stillness as if it would have alerted every badger along the two hundred miles of the Highland edge. It certainly silenced the scufflers.

I turned my attention back to the roe deer, infuriated by my careless habit of taking my binoculars off my neck so that I have to lay them down before I use my hands for anything else. I focussed on the willow and the doe, or rather the willow where the doe had been. Very much in the manner of the osprey's ability to appear mysteriously in the middle of the sky, the doe has the ability to materialise in the midst of a clearing, or dematerialise leaving no hint that she had ever been. If I had crossed to the willow I would have found the stems of the new leaves bitten through, her coffee bean droppings and her twin-slot foot-fall in a bare patch of badger-scuffed ground. The night grew quiet and chill, and when the tawny owl cast off from a forest spruce and glided on stiff wings across the clearing to perch in the oak at my back, I took my own leave of the hillside, hugging the clearing edge, walking away through the darkening rides to the car, to the four-gated mile of track and the hour's drive home under a full moon and a sky which was beginning to hold the night-long pallor of midsummer.

Two nights later, I was in the wood by six, quartering the clearing painstakingly, avoiding the badger paths with my unwelcome man-scent, seeking out the roe calf. There had been no sight of the doe although I had diverted laboriously to come on the clearing from downwind. I stood tree-still for half-an-hour at the forest edge before stepping into the open ground. But the wraith of her was by the willow again when I least expected it. She saw and scented and heard me, barked her command to the unseen calf and bounded loudly for the ride, advertising herself and her going. She stopped at the end of the ride and looked back down her spine in that characteristically roe fashion, as though she were assessing the impact of her ruse on her tormentor. I stood still and watched her watching me. In the glasses, she shone. Her summer chestnut coat was at its brand new glossiest best, with no lingering trace of winter's presbyterian grey-brown nor the grey muffler at her throat. And now that the calf was born she was slim and sleek and perfect. So she stood and she shone and she was wild and in her element, and I thought her fine. But I troubled her. She stepped away and bent low and, without breaking her stride, she passed into the dark embrace of the forest spruces under their lowest branches. She had done all she could do. Now she trusted to nature and her calf's instinct for stillness.

I cast quietly around for half an hour finding nothing among the deepest, tallest undergrowth, but when finally I found the calf it lay in the open on a patch of dead bracken. All that moved was the working black tip of her button nose.

Bambi did its job well, caricaturing the charm of the creature but not really exaggerating much. At a few feet away there is no more arresting and affecting sight in nature. The face, like a kitten or a puppy, is short and stubby and perfect, rich brown, but pale under the chin and above the eyes, almost black on the muzzle and the brow. The cocked ears are as white inside as they are black outside. The eyes big and black, lashes preposterously long and pretty. The coat is a browner shade of its mother's finery, but the spine and either flank wear broken stripes of small white patches from rump to neck. Below the flank stripes, the white patches look more haphazard and the background tone of the coat darkens. The legs, those implausible spindles Bambi had so much trouble with on ice ('Kinda wobbly aintcha?'), are folded impecccably beneath. I photographed quickly, talking as softly and reassuringly as I could, moving slowly, keeping always a distance of five or six feet away. The calf did not flinch, not once. But... the fundamental 'but'...

If you are fortunate enough to stumble on such a creature, and if you are unfamiliar with the ways of roe deer, there is a single unbreachable commandment: DO NOT TOUCH. To disregard it is unforgivable. The doe will abandon the calf which carries taint of human scent, and an abandoned calf does not live long and does not die pleasantly. Remember too that what you are looking at is not abandoned. You have come across not a farmyard pet but a wild animal behaving like a wild animal, and defending itself against your incomprehensible intrusion the only way it knows how. Somewhere nearby a doe watches you fearfully.

I left for the beech and the long wait for the badgers to emerge. It was good to see doe and calf together near the top of the sett an hour later, but I confess that I did not see the doe return, nor the reunion with her offspring.

I did not expect the badgers to be out for at least another two hours, although there is nothing less certain than predicting nature. I kept half an eye on the sett and stayed more or less still while I scribbled in a pad and watched the rest of the wild world at work. Tree pipits were firing themselves high into the air from the willow, then parachuting down, cock-tailed and singing.

It was a spectacular ritual for such an unprepossessing slip of a thing, and not without risk either, considering the hawk tribes which haunt the place. The hurtling display had been going on for twenty minutes when a hill-quartering kestrel slipped out of its hovering daydream and cut a fast shallow dive down over the spruces and came to an airy standstill directly over the willow, looking down. The kestrel is not much of a birder, being more thirled to the vole-pounce, but the pipits simply vanished altogether and at once. The hoverer was gone in ten seconds, and was no sooner out of sight beyond the spruces than the pipits were spurting up like fireworks, sliding down their songs, carefree as badgers.

The wind was better, a thin north-easterly which blew the steam from my coffee reassuringly back into my face as I drank, but it was not enough of a wind to deter the midges, nor to prevent clouds of drizzling rain from snagging on the hills and hissing down on the emergent bracken. The last two days of strong sun and rain had advanced the bracken alarmingly and unfurled the hawthorn blossom. The wind also brought me that blessing, that hawthorn scent which is the one great benefit to the wildlife watcher of the advance of summer on such a hillside.

There was the woodcock again, the same bird, identifiable by the curious rhythms of his call, his Ellingtonian tendencies meticulously syncopated, somewhere near the top of the sett. On the basis of past performance, I could expect him now to turn right at the top of the sett into the ride, and of course, having anticipated the move, he held his course and I lost him against the spruces as he beat doggedly uphill. I sat in the shadows, in the darkening, dripping shadows, and shrugged.

The evening felt as if it were getting away from me. In such circumstances, you start willing the hands on your watch round to nine o'clock, guessing that there was no chance of anything much happening before that. The watch is in on the evening's game, though, and the hands begin to dawdle. The date said 1 June, and a less June-like night would not have been easy to contrive. Nine o'clock came and went without so much as a syllable of thrush to relieve the gloom. By 9.30 p.m. I had reached the point of giving myself 15 minutes more. Three-and-a-half hours was a reasonable shift in this weather. I had the roe to show for it, and if the rain continued to thicken there was little prospect of badgers emerging at all. Then the grass started to wave.

I have watched the passage of the big boar through the grasses, a decisive progress accompanied by that volume of sound which suggests fearlessness. This was different. The grass did not wave so much as waver, and the grass-waverer, whatever it was, steered an erratic and infuriatingly slow course downhill towards the burn from the far side of the sett. The grass and the bracken on that flank of the slope was at its thickest, completely obscuring the waverer, but on it came, rustling as it wavered. It did not sound like badger. The noises were not care-free enough, the scope of the movement not big enough, the gestures not grand enough. Then the grasses parted at the foot of the slope twenty yards from my tree to reveal two nose-down trundlers travelling a notch above hedgehog speed, two grey sacks each with a perfectly finished miniaturised badger head at what I took to be the front. The cubs!

Something like an electric shock possessed me. Alone on that sodden grey hillside, with the rain and the midges doling out their stultifying regime in unrelieved dollops of oppressive irritation, I felt as if I had been electrically supercharged. Every nerve-end crackled into life. I muttered:

'You beauties!'

Here, without warning, and out of the midst of an adversity of tedium, I was confronted with my troubled badger endeavours' crowning sense of purpose. I watched these two small and all but shapeless shambling creatures in a state of suppressed ecstasy. I was immediately drunk on a thoroughly unprofessional cocktail of relief and throat-catching emotion.

It was all as short-lived as it was euphoric. At the sudden sound of a shotgun in the field beyond the burn (some farmer on a rabbiting ploy), the cubs galvanised into the perfect over-the-top parody of every cub which ever tottered out into its first light of day. They spun round, ran, collided, fell over, jumped up and, brushing shoulders and then bouncing off one another, they barged back into the grasses, hell-bent on the dark sanctuary of the sett, and were gone.

I looked down in disbelief at the glasses and the camera in my hands. The supercharged nerves were numb. I was a child of five handed a wondrous balloon only to have the neighbourhood bully stick a pin in it, leaving me holding the useless string in my hand. Because there was nothing else to be done, I blamed the conspiracy. I told it aloud:

'If this is your idea of a joke, it's not bloody funny.'

I had had enough for the night, but the night had not finished with me yet. I was packing away the camera, pulling on a waterproof jacket for the walk out when the cubs came back. Without fuss or fanfare they were rustling over the slope below the sett. One inched towards me across the bottom of the slope. The second was nosing a furrow downhill. If they held their courses for long they would collide about the time they fell over my right boot. Each was oblivious of the other, oblivious of everything other than the next green inch of undergrowth. They were about eighteen inches long, dark grey, shapeless as pyjama cases, except that each shapelessness was towed along by a perfectly formed miniaturised badger head.

I had never seen badger cubs before. I had not known there were cubs here. I had set myself up to watch the boar's entrance in the hope of photographing him. Now as I tried to keep track of both cubs by swivelling my eyes and keeping my head still, I saw the boar emerge and pose perfectly for three seconds. I dared not risk movement, not now, so he posed unphotographed, then without a glance at the cubs, he left.

The contouring cub reached the boar's hole and vanished. The downhill cub crept nearer. I pressed against the fallen trunk, became tree. The cub was close enough to be heard, small snuffles and grunts as it explored the world just below the surface of the grasses with his nose and his forefeet. It sneezed once. The noise made me think of a childhood pet budgie which sneezed after drinking.

Inexorably, inch by beetle-gluttonous inch, the cub began to change direction, curving across the slope to within ten feet of me, then edging away towards the tall bracken. The boar had gone. The other cub had gone. I would not lose this one. The cub had shown no sign of acknowledging my presence. I risked everything and followed as close as I dared.

In the next fifteen minutes I covered perhaps one hundred yards on all fours with a camera in one hand. The bracken towered over the badger cub which poked and prodded and nosed at its roots. My face parted curtains of midges. I began photographing. The camera clicked and flashed but the cub barely noticed. Only once, when I was within six feet of its turned back did it spin round and hiss. I held still and it snuffled off again, nosing away the inches.

I could take no more of the midges which had begun to fill my nose and ears. I left the little one to its darkening underworld and stepped back along my own trail through the woods. I walked slowly and softly, lightly burdened by a growing wonderment.

Back at the car, I met the farmer walking his small tribe of dogs.

'Did you see anything tonight?' he asked.

'There are two cubs.'

'Two! That's good, eh?'

'Good enough for me,' I said.

II

Old Moon Face

T HE WIND WAS WRONG for the beech, a niggling little south-westerly which would push my scent right across the full range of the sett entrances. There was nothing for it but the willow. I had tested the tree on my first exploration of the sett and found it wanting. I was not looking forward to an evening in its spindly embrace. It stood no more than a dozen yards from the top holes of the sett, and it leaned towards them, commanding a fair view of the top half of the clearing but nothing at all of the bottom half, nor of the great majority of the sett's entrances. It demanded a standing vigil – both feet on a flattened bend in the trunk about three inches wide – and a precarious clasp to flimsy branches which swayed at the least provocation from the wind. But it was better than nothing. It might give me a better idea of where the badgers went when they left the clearing – as long as they left from the top, of course.

The usual cast of players strolled on and off – roe, robin, woodcock, noises off from the cuckoo – but it looked as if it was turning into one of those inexplicably blank badger nights when, at almost 10 o'clock, I saw a small badger squeeze under the fence just uphill from the beech and pad along beside the burn. It was in the glasses for a moment, then wobbled unprettily over a broken-down drystane dyke to the water's edge where it vanished. I was sure, or at least as sure as I could be at a hundred yards and given the tremulous nature of my perch, that it was one of the cubs. The adventurous independence of the cubs at eight or nine weeks old (April births are not rare this far north) is impressive. Their mustelline curiosity and their badger courage, their robust attitude to life and all its obstacles – all these seem to be in place from the first. I had no way of knowing whether or not the adults were particularly lacking in parental responsibility at this sett or whether the cubs were particularly outgoing, but it was clear that the cubs' independence was encouraged and relished.

Could I catch up with the badger at the burn?

The thought no sooner lodged than I was jumping gratefully down from the willow, recklessly disregarding the prospect of other badgers on the lower half of the sett, skirting the clearing along its topmost edge and coming on the burn well upstream. Then in wellies and waterproof trousers I simply walked down the burn, wary among the loose boulders, eyes working the banks for a shroud-shape in the shadows and its betraying white face. I wanted to know where it went. I wanted to watch it confront its wider world. I wanted to be in on its secret life beyond the sett, and for once, for one night at least, it proved easier than I thought.

Somehow the cub had not only negotiated the lumpy and ragged-edged obstacle of the broken-down dyke (and much scratching on moss and lichen and even rock suggested it was a regular crossing for all the badgers) but it had also crossed the burn. That amazed me. I felt the volume of water in the pool where I stood tugging at my boots. I thought of the size of the creature which had just crossed here or hereabouts and I could not understand why it had not been tossed a rock step or two downstream with a skinful of broken bones for its trouble. But there it was instead, nearing the top of easier grass slopes on the far side of the burn. It stood there on the top of the bank for a few seconds, a tiny silhouette, a scrap of the hillside, looking of no more account than the end of a stout branch thrown down in a gale. Then it moved off and I stepped from the burn and followed.

Something of a sense of the ridiculous began to creep into the night. I am half an inch short of six feet, and thirteen-and-a-half stones, and I was attempting to pursue and remain inconspicuous to a badger cub ten weeks old at the most, eighteen inches long at the most and half as high, and which almost certainly did not know where it was going.

It was not hard to understand why such a creature would pause at the top of the bank. There had been the first dark underground weeks, incomprehensible to us and to most of nature for that matter, for most of us are born into the daylight world. Then there were the first stumblings around the sett followed by the first forays out into the closed-in tree-shadowed limits of the clearing. Then there would be the first crossing of the stream (this could easily have been that first crossing) and the climb up the grass bank. How the first sight of the landscape beyond the burn must have widened the eyes of the mite and stopped it in its adventuring tracks. Suddenly the land is wide and bright and dipping tremendously, the grass cropped short, rough pasture knee-high to the cub, the sky vast and coloured, and at the centre of everything the cone of a distant mountain. The badger cub cresting that small green rise would also feel for the first time the brush of an unhindered wind. It would be a soulless beast indeed (and a badger is not one of these) which could fail to stop and be impressed by its first sight of all that.

And then, from the same low-slung point of view, what might the badger cub make of sheep?

There was my cub, not twenty yards uphill, making steady progress, stopping often to sniff, hugging the field edge as though its bright green spaces were too daunting. The first lamb spotted it and came bounding over bravely. Most likely, lamb had never seen badger either. It stopped ten feet short of the cub, which appeared not to have noticed it. But then it did notice, and in a gesture which doubtless established utterly the relationship between badger and sheep for as long as it would matter to these two creatures in particular, it spun round and hissed. I recognised the same defiant greeting with which it accosted my camera in the bracken. The lamb turned and ran, bleating to the sanctuary of its mother's udder.

The cub was also about to make another discovery, one which would confer on the field the status of Valhalla. One deft scoop of a clawed foot and one brief foray of a questing snout in the soft earth and it had tapped into a lifetime's supply of what it is a badger loves best in all the wild world: worms. As far as I could tell from my carefully discreet pursuit in and out of the tree-lined edge of the field, it ate four more in about fifty yards, but the same fifty yards took the best part of ten minutes to cover. A badger cub feeding on worms is not a spectacular progress. Not only must the worms be found but every other square inch has to scented and sifted and tested for food or danger, or just to satisfy an insatiable curiosity, the badge of its tribe.

Somewhere up that sloping field in the last of the light something triggered off a considered assessment in the badger cub of its solitary vulnerability. I saw and heard nothing, but the hunter-wanderer suddenly turned tail and ran. It ran as you never saw anything run before. Suddenly the creature had legs, its hair seemed to stand on end, and as it ran, no part of it seemed to be in contact with the ground. As well as worms, the cub was tasting fear for the first time. Twenty yards from me it swerved left into the trees, half ran and half rolled down the bank, splashed and boulder-hopped through the burn without pause and was last seen clambering the wall back into the sett clearing. A spectacular progress.

I resisted the impulse to follow again and decided instead to wait and watch and stay still. I wanted to know what had terrified the cub, but also, after days locked into the psychology of this and other badger setts, I was enjoying that cool and airy corner of the hillside. The wide tumbling summer green of the field, the pale yellow sky, the grey and cloud-smoking cone of the mountain distance...I breathed them all in.

It did not do, I rebuked myself, to grow so immersed in the badgers' head-down world that I neglected instincts of my own. Not for the first time I recognised that, although I had become mesmerised by badgers in the wild, I was less than wholly at ease in their shut-in dusky woods. It had helped shifting the focus of my badger watching to this preferred landscape, but it had not solved the ever-present problem. They were primarily creatures of the dark, and when the shortest nights propelled them reluctantly into the last hours of daylight, that compulsory aspect of badger-watching propelled me out into that season of nature I like least: summer. Even so, I had set the rules myself, and what warmed me to the task was the eye-opening of it, the discovering of that which I had not discovered before, the slow unfolding of furtive lives, the painstaking task of the jigsaw-puzzler who knows that at best he will finish with half a picture, but who knows too that it is the puzzling, the piece-gathering which is the chief satisfaction, not the finishing of the picture. Even Ernest Neal himself has acknowledged – to my grateful satisfaction – that with badgers the picture is far from complete. With that wholly praiseworthy concession in the forefront of my mind, I had to promise myself that I, as the rawest of badger beginners, should not expect too much too soon.

In the high corner of the field where a shelter belt met the trees of the burn's gorge at right angles, there was a pale stirring, and an old familiar shape from my Angus youth laid the quietest wings in the wilds on the night air. At once the badger cub's discomfort was explained. It had just tasted the elixir of earth worms, looked up (as far up as a badger cub looks, which admittedly is not far) and seen its first ghost, the eerily unnerving long-winged twilit silence of old moon-face, the barn owl.

The mind's eye turns somersaults at how a head-on hunting barn owl must look to an inches-off-the-ground head-down eyes-up badger cub trying to come to terms with the wide open world and the taste of earth worms at the same time. A badger life may never know headier moments than these, trembling in the safe dark of the sett, nursing fearfully the new knowledge. The cub would not know, not yet, that the barn owl is a mouser, that even on the cub's first foray the barn owl already considers it too ferocious a foe. The cub will learn that soon enough, learn too that he has nothing to fear in the wild, nothing other than the tall two-legged tree-shaped one that walks on his roof and sours his paths with a dreaded scent.

Owl and badger have much in common. Both are reluctant in daylight. Like the badger, the barn owl is a shadow creature with a white mask pinned to a book page by a camera flash, the light illuminating the shadow and throwing an owl. The true owl, like the true badger, is the colourless one, the daylit image not to be trusted. Even the twilit one has begun to fade and pale, abandoning substance and becoming a night wraith.

I have known the wraith one since earliest memory. Childhood began in the last street in town in Dundee. On the other side of the road was a farm then, and it was all long enough ago for the farm to have a stackyard. Barn owls went in among the haystacks ghosting rats to death (or so I was told once by the farmer, a coarse creature and as filthy as his farm, and that amounted to a wheen of filth).

The miracle of the owls in such a dirty grey place was their whiteness. I can remember them now only as creatures of the winter night, perched on the haystack poles while unseen hordes of geese cruised loudly through the blackness. I can still feel the peculiar touch of the poles, the smooth fur of frost and the crinkled brittle bark beneath. I can still see the owl swinging low round a stack and seeing me crouched there and both of us turning and fleeing fast in opposite directions. No owl was going to ghost me to death.

The farm is long gone. Stackyards have become extinct and the barn owl has retreated back and back, ghosted to death himself by a changed agriculture. Not just the stackyards have gone, but stone barns too, and hedgerows and copses and much else which was to the barn owl's liking, and which held farming closer to nature and farmers closer to the land.

The farmer calls it progress, and who's to argue with him? Barn owls, perhaps, and humans like me who would prefer smaller grain mountains, and more moon-faces to trouble the first explorations of a June badger on the Highland Edge.

12

Dream Enough For Me

BRACKEN IS THE CURSE of summer on the Highland Edge. The osprey wood becomes all but impenetrable. By late June, the bank is jungly enough to swallow the roe doe as soon as she steps away from my appearance by the burn. The late spring blossoms of the wild hyacinth and hawthorn were done, their mingled fragrances lost to the oppressive stench of bracken. I battered my way up to that single hole where my Highland Edge badger trail had begun. Fronds flicked in my face and the flies rose in droning squadrons. It was hot and still.

The hole had grown immense. It looked as if the bank's loose and sandy soil had caved in at the mere passage of the animal, but although the entrance was clean, the spoil heap was old and the tracks through the bracken were not trodden down enough to suggest regular badger traffic. I was sure now that the hole was just an occasional stop-over. Because of the way the tracks radiated north and south from the top of the bank, I was just as sure that it served badgers from both the osprey wood below and the hillside above.

I was too hot and my shirt was wet, like clingfilm on my back. I had climbed to the top of the bank and flicked a broken off bracken frond at the smudge of flies before my face while I tried to focus the glasses and keep them still with one hand. Far across the wood, and 150 feet above the ground, the female osprey was also feeling the heat. She had left her eggs and was standing on the outermost edge of the eyrie. She stood tall and pale like a weathercock on the spire of the wood. Nature makes few more beautiful gestures. Two trees to the west, her mate stood on the one higher perch in the wood and was looking at the sky. The ospreys had company, and company is what an osprey likes least. Usually they can outfly the kind of company which turns up – stroppy crows, homing gulls, cantankerous herons, that kind of thing. They even have the edge over the neighbourhood buzzards when it comes (as often it does) to a dogfight, an edge honed by the control of its hunting technique. Only a peregrine falcon is a more exquisite stooper than an osprey, and buzzards tend to dive for cover when an osprey gets above them. But now the ospreys had the kind of company which poses the one serious threat in their patch of sky – two more ospreys.

The female on the eyrie put her head back and threw the challenge of her alarm call at her mate. Not her screechiest protest but a lower-pitched preliminary. ('Lower pitched' is a relative term: all the osprey's repertoire is couched in thin soprano shades, not pretty, and not worthy of the bird's many graces, a flaw it shares with eagles and their incongruous terrier yaps.) The male's response was to rock back into a tall vertical stance, clutching the very highest inch of that vast fir, wings held high. Then the wings began to beat very slowly, a gesture which I had not seen before. It carried unmistakable tones of menace.

The intruders sailed closer, gliding high, infringing the eyrie's airspace. The shrieker raised her voice and her pitch. Her mate joined in – higher still, a hideous scratch – then he flew and the treetop rocked to the kicking thrust of his take-off. He dipped down behind the screen of giant firs only to re-emerge climbing furious and fast and aimed directly at the lower of the two new birds. Whether the intruders were young and inexperienced birds which assumed the attack from below was bluff, or whether the gliding bird was merely careless or slow, there is no way of knowing. The eyrie male flew on at the same undeviating angle of his power climb. At the last moment, when I was convinced the gliding bird would wing-dip aside, the attacker thrust forward his feet and, still climbing, smashed into the belly of his victim.

The intruder bounced backwards up the sky, then fell. The male dived after it, chased by the second intruder which swooped into the melée.

A new screech from below – as the dogfight fell towards her, the female rose from the eyrie tree to defend it, holding a defensive circle just above the eyrie and its precious eggs.

For ten minutes three ospreys corkscrewed above the wood while the female held tight, calling all the encouragement her mate needed. He was clever and more experienced than the gatecrashers and more than a match for their combined efforts. No other blow was struck but he turned tighter, climbed faster and, having gained high positions, he fell like a rock. The inevitability of the outcome did not diminish the thrill of the spectacle. I have watched ospreys jousting before, many times, but have seen nothing like that performance, and when the intruders finally pulled out and headed for the loch with the eyrie male snapping at their tails, I wanted to stand and applaud.

His mate settled again on the rim of the nest, and when he returned half an hour later, a trout glittered in his feet and the call from her was a very different one. Ten minutes later he brought her the uneaten half and they changed places. He stood guard on the nest, she used his perch to eat the fish from her foot. When she slipped back on to the nest from below she held a branch in her feet and fussed it into position. The male meanwhile had circled the tree twice before gliding slowly in just above the eyrie to perch on her back. With the June sun beating down, and the treetop doubtless rocking in time, the hero of the hour mated with his distressed damsel. All this in the ninety minutes or so since I had decided to abandon any idea of watching ospreys in that fly-strewn heat. In those same ninety minutes the flies had diminished to a barely noticeable irritant. When you are dealing with the ospreys of the heavens you don't concern yourself with the creatures of the dungheap.

I remembered the day I came back to look for the returning ospreys and found the badger hole as well. I daydreamed badger cubs beneath my feet and osprey fledglings over my head and I knew I was daydreaming. But the living reality nature coughed up on a hot afternoon at the end of June was dream enough for me.

I waved to the ospreys, an altogether futile gesture but a habit I have got into ... wildlife or landscape which moves or thrills me is rewarded with a wave. I wave to the Cairngorms from the A9, Skye from the ferry, almost any swan anywhere, and I wave to ospreys from quarter of a mile away.

I had decided to set aside three consecutive evenings to try and pin down a badger sett in the osprey wood, my unsatisfied curiosity getting the better of my unease at the vaguely claustrophobic nature of that old rambling and overgrown place. The weather was settled, the time of year ideal with almost endless daylight and badgers at their most visible.

The badger path (which is also a roe deer path, fox path, rabbit path) inclines away east down a long gentle slope. Its fringing bracken was already chest-high, and because I was moving again and moving deeper into the wilder acres of that landscape, I slipped on a light bracken-green jacket. I was as camouflaged as any walking man can be.

The doe was browsing out in the open a hundred yards ahead. If she saw me at all, she did not see my meaning. She heard, though, and watched with her ears, leaning them towards me. She put her nose to the air but the wind told her nothing. She relaxed again and browsed. While she ate, head down in tall grasses, I moved. When she looked up, I froze. So I came to within thirty yards of her, put the glasses on her and admired what I saw.

Her face, mostly black, was enlivened by two 'badger' stripes of her rich chestnut coat. She cocked her ears forward again, facing me, then moved one of them carefully away in a controlled flap to the side and behind; then she flicked it forward again. Every nerve, her every sense, was at work; her jaw moved rhythmically on the summer-sweet grass and birch leaves. She half turned and walked towards a fence enclosing a field of rough pasture. She took the fence in a single perfect step-jump from a standing start, and if I had seen nothing else all day, the image I froze of her in mid-air, glossy in the early evening sun, would have been a good day's work to take home.

She began to graze again, and now that I was deprived of good cover, I stalked on my hands and knees to the fence and watched again.

All I was watching was a roe deer going about its everyday business, being its own wild and relaxed self, and by every set of human-defined aesthetic standards, being beautiful. It is that such a thing can happen with the deer unaware of your presence which makes the difference, to know that you have worked for it and it has briefly come off and you have eavesdropped on nature with its defences down. In any final analysis of my nature-writer's life, there is nothing better.

A ragged-winged heron surprised me from behind, flying low over my head, then low over the roe's, startling her too. Then a farm vehicle pulled up far across the field and she turned to look at that, and when the gate opened and the farmer ushered in a herd of cattle, she retraced her steps and leaped the fence again. She ignored the sounds which were part of her world: traffic on the quiet road half a mile away, a shepherd's distant shout, dog bark, but my knee inadvertently crushing a cushion of dead bracken whipped her head up and she trotted away. Perhaps I would catch up with her when I walked out. I stood and slotted back into the badger trail.

The path crossed the flat ground towards the burn, crossed the burn by an old slatted wooden estate bridge, after which it split in two and grew immediately indistinct. The best of the woodland was here, an open, airy birchwood which climbed and thickened to a vast and voluptuous mass of rhododendrons that skirted a stand of great oaks. The buzzards nested in one of these and sallied forth to squabble with the ospreys. Beyond the oaks the wood darkened and grew dismal where an old untended plantation shut out the light. Facing the plantation was a bank which held an old sett, as untended as the trees. I had walked there before and didn't care if I never saw it again.

My hopes rested with a piece of open ground below the rhododendrons. It was fringed on one side with willows and petered out among the birches on the others. The bracken was still no more than knee high here, and early in May I had found several patches of bare earth thick with badger hairs and willow catkins. I had tracked the paths back to the willow trees and reasoned that foraging badgers caught the catkins on their underfur and scratched them out in the moult. Certainly there were enough bare patches and trails to suggest several badgers. Now, although the moult would be over, I could find none of them. The trails still cut through the bracken and looked busy enough. I leaned against a birch tree and let the place soak in, and asked myself again where the sett might be. It was in none of the obvious banks for I had checked them all more than once. It was not on the flat ground, nor among the oaks or the huge firs. The rhododendrons blazed violent clouds of purple all along the top of the bank which faced me, and in two or three places they spilled down the bank an impenetrable mass. The thought had no sooner formed than I spoke aloud the words:

'Unless . . . you are a badger.'

The path at my feet led all the way and vanished straight into the bottom of one of those downhill spillages of purple. A flattened path ran up one side of the mass of bushes and then dipped back downhill into a

steep brackeny wedge which the rhododendrons had all but sur-
rounded. The path tunnelled straight in among the twiggy morass of
the understorey. I lay flat and peered into its unwelcoming gloom.
I couldn't advance six inches, but a badger could. And did by the look
of things. Whether or not there was a sett, of course ...

I backed out, stamped a sightline through the bracken from the top
of the bank then sat there at the other end of it. If anything moved in
the rhodies, or moved out of them, or crossed anywhere in half a square
mile of woodland, I would see it. I sensed my triumph already.

I watched the sky empty of cloud, then of colour. I watched a
woodcock thatch its airspace, crossing again and again. I felt the touch
of air frost and blessed it for the midges faded at once. I saw a ground
mist stir down on the burn, a tiny colourless pocket of stuff which
inexorably grew but lay only along the half-mile straight of the burn
three or four feet above the ground. I sat through four hours before I
gave up, badgerless, at midnight. I walked back along the burn's bank,
wading through the chest-high mist, my footfall the only sound apart
from the punctuations of owl and sleepless cuckoo. Such a stillness! It
lay on the wood, a benevolent blanket, a peace so deep it was almost
touchable. I stopped to get a deeper sense of it, noticing what it felt like,
what it sounded like, what it looked like. To the west and north – the
only sky I could see – there was no cloud and the heavens were as
unblemished white as a snowfield in an Arctic winter. I walked on, and
at my second footfall two mallard ducks burst up through the mist.

That moment has replayed in my mind a thousand times, and every
time (always in the slowest of slow motions) I see the duck heads and
backs pushing the mist aside as they rise vertically, I see the mist roll
away from their backs and the water fall in shed droplets as the wings
slice forward and back, fall from their dangling orange feet and hiss
back through the mist on to the still water. And I feel my heart jump
clear through my mouth and hover somewhere above my head while
the rest of me takes an involuntary backwards step where a booted foot
snags in a small hole and I sit heavily in a ditch.

The following two nights were equally badgerless and the wood
hugged its badger secret to itself. I wrote them off to experience and

headed off back along my man-trail a mile up the hill. I wondered if the ospreys knew where the badgers were.

There is among my circle of acquaintances a great friend, a badger man older than I and wiser by far in the ways of the brock. We are habituated in the art of leaning over a bar table well furnished with glasses of the island malt-fire, his unfailingly the Islay of it, mine swithering between the Skye and the Orkney of it. As often as not, the crack is of wildlife adventures, our own and other people's and when it's his turn, as often as not the crack is of badgers. He smiled his acknowledgement of a refill and said:

'You might like to use this. This was my first badger.'

I sharpened the pencil point in my mind and listened.

'There's a place in the Lake District, a place I climbed once when I was a lad. It was one of those mad youthful escapades you survive and learn from. Often when I passed the place after that I would stop there and look up and shudder. On one such occasion, years after, I was driving past and stopped to look up at the screes.'

He shuddered again, the climb revisited.

'There was a steep field just below the screes, and in it was what looked like a badger – or at least it was what looked like what I thought a badger would look like – but it was the middle of the day. I assumed it was dead, so I walked up to it none too cautiously. Well, you don't care if you think it's dead. I was only a few feet away when I realised it was *snoring*. The bloody thing was asleep!'

Was it lying in some kind of day nest, I asked, for I had heard tell of such temporary badger accommodation, but never seen it myself.

'No. Nothing. It was just lying curled up out in the field, out in the sun, and it was fast a-bloody sleep. No day nest. Nothing! Just there. It was as if it had just lain down and dozed off! I walked right up to it and touched it. Nothing! I touched it again and it woke, looked round, got up, shook itself, looked at me with an expression that said "What the ... ?" and trotted away, chattering to itself the way they do, mumble mumble mumble. I watched it go, and I daresay my mouth was hanging open.'

That had got him started, and having started he was quickly in his stride. He always makes good listening when he's in his stride.

He moved to south-west Scotland after that, a cottage up a track, and by then he was hooked on badgers and delighted to see one on his track as he was driving home late at night.

'I had to find out where they were of course, and I followed their tracks. Eventually I found the sett near a neighbouring cottage. I told the neighbour, an old fellow, what I'd found because I hoped he'd be able to tell me about them. It was a very old sett and well used. He said:

'"Never seen a badger."

'I said: "How long have you lived here?"

'He said: "Eighty years, son." '

My mind went back to my own farmer neighbour at the Holly Glen. 'There's nae badgers here,' he had pronounced, and I fancied them hugging themselves six feet beneath his boots. I suppose the moral is that you only see if you are accustomed to the looking.

The Ayrshire years gave my friend his best badger-watching, and there was a certain tree with a set of small step ladders next to it. 'They're probably still there. I certainly never took them away when I left.' That was his watching tree, and one night he watched this:

'When I heard the boat train from Stranraer go past – that was the signal. They always seemed to come out just after that. Why the train, heaven knows. Some people say it's the woodcock that brings them out ...'

Aye, and some people say baloney to all that, and I'm one of them, but never mind, where were we ... ?

'The train had just gone when a cat came wandering through the sett, and right under the badger platform it stopped and peed, then it wandered on. The boar came to the entrance a few minutes later, cautious as ever, scenting the wind as usual. Then you could almost sense the change in attitude, almost see the nose wrinkling in disgust. He could hardly bring himself to put his face out. Again and again he would get as far as the entrance, scent the air, and go back.

'Eventually he came out, right out on the platform and stood there. You could see the nose working, as if appalled by what it was smelling. He came down, nose to the ground, right to where the cat had peed, and when his nose got *there*, it was like he had walked straight into an electric fence. He *sprang* back, all four feet off the ground, right back into the sett, one backward bounce. I nearly fell out of the tree laughing. Then, while he was still there, the cubs came pushing past him and skipped over the same offensive spot without so much as a second glance, or a sniff. Badgers? They're the greatest!' He looked down at the glasses.

'One for the ditch?'

Back at the couped-over beech, testing the sightline I had carved out in the bracken by turning up a couple of hours early and stamping down a six-feet wide furrow between the boar's preferred entrance and the beech, my own preferred watching place. It would have to be wider, that furrow, if I was going to continue to watch here. The bracken in mid-July was head-high when I walked through and as thick with flies as blossom on a May hawthorn, a hellish passage. All I would be able to tell now was when a badger emerged and which way it went – and that was invariably left anyway. After that it would be a case of waiting until it came down to the more open ground near the burn. But not tonight. By 10.30 p.m. nothing had stirred, and in the hot still breathlessness of the night, and tormented by midges, I had had enough.

The forest ride is dark at such a time of night, even in midsummer. Moving against a dark frontier of spruces, wearing my dark badger-watching clothes, and walking slowly and carefully, there is always a chance, especially when the wind is with you, of catching something unawares. It does not do to relax when leaving the sett clearing just because the official part of the watch is over. The fact that I did not see the badger go or hear it stir does not necessarily mean that it has not gone, not stirred. Two or three hundred yards into the ride I heard the grass move unnaturally and stopped at once in mid-stride. The ride at that spot was about ten yards wide and bisected by an old low dyke. The spruces crowded in on either side. Grass, perhaps three feet long, on the far side of the dyke was wavering. I let my eyes rest on it without trying too hard to make sense of it at once. In such gloom the eyes like to find their own definition of things. By the time the grass moved again, all was as sharp as it could be, and as it moved a grey shape hardened through it. A badger face was staring at me.

I have never learned to take that face for granted, never learned to be unimpressed by its bearishness, particularly when it is the broad head of such a heavyweight boar. The half-light magnified him again, and the whiteness of his face was the whitest badger I ever saw. He sat back.

Just like that, he sat back. He did not run or panic or hide. He looked straight at me and he sat. It was as if he had seen or heard (both probably) my presence, but because of the darkness and the tree curtains behind me, and my own dark garb, he was unsure what to make of it. By now my scent must have grown familiar to him around the sett and along my man-trail, and as no harm had come to him because of it, perhaps he was no longer wary of it. In any case the wind was in my face, and if I had been a scenting kind of creature, I could have caught his drift rather than wait for the grasses to move. Whatever, we were what we were and we faced each other across a few yards of forest ride and a broken dyke. And, the better to see and hear me, he sat back ...

The sitting had a second purpose. I recognised it at once. When he had seen me first, he was side on and low to the ground, and his head was turned sideways. Now he faced me directly and his body was massed and curved behind him, and being the kind of heftily-muscled thing he was, he looked three times the size of his side-on, low-slung self.

He shot a sidelong glance to the shadow of the dyke, then looked back at me. The grass moved again: the sow! She padded over to him and the grass opened before her and closed at her back. She went behind him, and half-hidden by his bulk she peered round his far shoulder. Then she trotted to the forest edge and stepped inside. He grunted and followed. I stood, unmoving, hoping against hope that the cubs were close by too and might answer some unheard summons. But the grass in the ride remained still. Two woodcocks hurtled up the ride, low overhead, matching each other, wingbeat for wingbeat. In a curious variation on the predictable theme of woodcock-speak, both birds squeaked continuously and neither croaked.

The cracking of underfoot twigs in the spruces turned my attention back to the badgers. They hadn't gone far, and I wondered if they might return. Then I wondered if I might lure them back. They were weasels, after all, and the one thing a weasel can't resist is something that will ensnare his curiosity. So from the crouching lee of the dyke, with just my head showing above it, I began to click my tongue and pop a finger against the inside of my mouth, whistle softly, anything I could think of which might fall curiously on listening ears without sounding remotely human. The twigs crackled just inside the trees. They certainly weren't leaving, but were they coming back? I clicked and popped and whistled some more and the twigs shifted and crackled. Just when I thought the idea was going nowhere, the whistling woodcocks returned and, with their whistles coinciding with my pops and clicks, the boar's face appeared almost on the ground under the very lowest branches of the spruces. Then the sow's face appeared beside it, two white masks in a wall of black trees. Then came the cubs!

For ten seconds, certainly no more, all four faces gleamed out of the forest at me, and it was all I could do to stifle a laugh. They were like nothing so much as characters from a puppet theatre. I see them now in my mind's eye. I will see them fifty years from now, if my God-of-the-wilds spares me that long, their image undimmed. It was the only time I had seen all four badgers together, and I had met them in the way I had always set as my highest ambition for meeting badgers, by chance out in their world, away from the sett, going about their business and just being.

I have never been completely comfortable with 'set-up' nature, luring wildlife with bait (peanuts or honey with badgers) to a certain place to produce a certain photograph; and much as I admire the work of such as Mike Tomkies from ingeniously-worked hides (so ingenious in his case that an eagle he was filming perched on his hide while he was inside, unaware that he was looking at her talons!) I find my own instincts best served when I can just go and become, as far as is humanly possible, a discreet fragment of the natural world. There is no greater reward for me than to encounter wildlife on those terms, for in such circumstances, that part of me which is still 'nature' comes to the fore and briefly dominates mind, eye, sensibility, and I think it dignifies the human breast, however momentarily.

The four faces beneath the trees withdrew, leaving blackness in their places. I heard the twigs crack back down towards the sett, and I listened until I could hear no more. I walked out to the car half a mile away, and as I walked I felt like a creature not quite in touch with the ground – something like a badger for example.

I considered one more night there, but first I would go in for an afternoon's hard labour, cutting a great swathe of bracken from the slope below the sett so that my beech tree perch could contemplate an avenue the badgers, especially the cubs, might use. So I went in and cut, and ended up at the beech dripping with perspiration from my exertions. Peering through fly-clouds, I looked at what I had cut and regretted the deed. Was it any different, I rebuked myself, from putting down bait? All I was doing was making things easier for myself, or at least less difficult. And what made me think a badger would use my man-made twenty-yards-wide pathway of felled bracken rather than its own padded down trail evolved through its wild year, and doubt-less laid down on the line of trails padded down by untold generations of badgers? My doubts were well founded. When I returned two nights later, it was to see the boar emerge and stand briefly in the moon-light at the top of my felled swathe. Then, for the first time, in all the occasions I had watched him over the spring and summer months, he turned not left across the top of my clearing but right, straight into the thickest bracken.

I drew my own private conclusions from that. I went back once more, in mid-September, and although he turned left with the sow close behind him, and I trailed them quietly up through the top of the sett towards the open hill, they slipped away from me in the highest spruces, and the contact felt broken. By then the mountain badgers had shown their bouldery place up for what it was, a temporary speculative venture. There, too, the bracken had grown head-high and effectively barred my way up to the higher ground where the mountain had burst open. I would wait for the clearer days of winter, and the next peregrine-scratched skies of another spring.

13
Why Badgers Die

T HERE IS EVIDENCE to suggest that badgers treat death with some respect, even dignity. Given the chance to die naturally, they do so mostly at the sett. There they are entombed by their own kind in a side tunnel or a chamber remote from the main runs. Perhaps the dying animal moves to such a last resting place itself and is walled in with earth once it had died. Perhaps the corpse is put there by badgers and then walled in. Either way, such burials are commonplace. Generations later the chamber may be re-worked by younger badgers and a skull will surface on a new spoil heap, but the animal's attitude to the death of a fellow reflects one more admirable and intriguing aspect of the dignified order which underpins badger society.

Then there is the question of 'funerals'. These are the stuff of rural lore in some parts of the country, uncorroborated and difficult to pin down. Yet they persist, and they are just as difficult to refute. The only references I have found involve adult badgers, and Ernest Neal himself is among those who have watched adults ignore a dead cub. Perhaps it may be that, if they do occur, funerals are reserved for dominant adults, a tribute from those lesser creatures of the sett which have benefited from their guidance and protection and ingenuity. Perhaps. The 'funerals' involve moving the corpse some distance, sometimes followed by burial or by covering it with leaves or bracken. Both possibilities require the co-operation of more than one badger, a planned and premeditated ritual. Authoritative accounts seem not to exist, and Neal himself is unconvinced if open-minded and wistfully optimistic that one day he may witness such a thing for himself.

There are not many ways for an adult badger to die. The infamous tuberculosis crisis in south-west England attracted nationwide head-

Badger cubs can often be seen in broad daylight

Fearless explorers, badger cubs will venture close

Play is an important element of badger life

Mother and cub out foraging in the wood at night

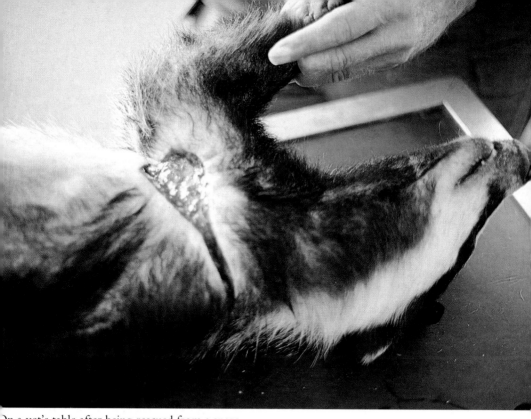

On a vet's table after being rescued from a snare

One of many victims of road accidents

The aftermath of the badger's raid on a wasps' nest

Badgers are back in the Holly Glen after an absence of several months

lines and outraged public opinion when infected setts were gassed. It appeared badgers were providing a reservoir for the disease and infecting cattle there, but it remains a rare example of a natural vulnerability in badgers. There are other natural deaths: parasites, fights with other badgers and occasional freak defeats. A small badger might be killed by a large fox, and, although I have never heard of such a thing, a wildcat would be a formidable foe for a Highland badger. But mostly when a badger dies it has been killed, directly or indirectly, by man. We kill badgers with our cars and trains, with night-lights and guns, with traps and poisons, and (in a curious perversion euphemistically called sport) with dogs.

Cars and trains we can do little enough about, for badgers will cross roads and railways, and purpose-built badger tunnels are expensive to instal, even during the construction of new roads. We can put up more warning signs but it is arguable that these simply advertise the presence of badgers and result in more disturbance or worse. They may ultimately take more lives than they save.

Death by poisoning, like so many other deaths by poisoning, will usually be the result of a badger eating bait poisoned to kill something else, foxes mostly. Poison does not discriminate, and neither do farmers and keepers who put it out in places where it might be taken by anything from a badger to a golden eagle or a buzzard to a bunny. Foxes do not have the badger's total protection in law, and who can prove the intention was ever otherwise? Gassing offers up the same excuse. The farmer thought he was killing foxes, and who knows whether he didn't want badgers near his cattle, or wanted to use the badgers' territory for his own purposes? (Sometimes the reclaiming is more subtle. One sett I watched in a wood between fields regularly offered up four adult badgers until, two days running, cattle were driven through the sett wood instead of round the side of it. The destruction was wholly effective. But now the badgers are trying again.) It still goes on, the fox is still the excuse, and there is often genuine surprise that it has been illegal to gas foxes now since 1989.

It is not illegal to set a snare, but the badger's strength is such that he can tow one around for weeks, maimed and enraged by pain. Policing the law is a different matter from inventing it, of course, and many a badger has died and continues to die quietly and in great pain, and only its human executioner knows why.

Then there is the question of sport which, its champions insist, must not be confused with cruelty. Of course things go wrong occasionally and a badger dies, but that's life, eh? Or death.

In my mind as I write is an image which haunts me. It was supposed to haunt. It haunts me the more because I was confronted by it a few months after I had reached the end of my badger year. By that time the badger had become a marvel in my eyes, and something of an unrequited friend.

The image was one which a television producer had used to conclude a two-part Channel 4 documentary on the activities of badger-baiting rings in England and Ireland, activities called 'sport'. I have adopted the word 'sport'. None of my words would get past my editor, nor my own respect for language.

A pro-badger, anti-baiting campaigner had insinuated himself into the midst of two rings of badger-digging sportsmen by means of a quite breathtaking combination of 'one-of-the-boys' deception and majestic lying. He also managed to film what he saw. It was a courageous programme and it turned my stomach.

There came the moment when the diggers and their dogs had so demented a badger that one of the sportsmen was able to grab it by the tail and hold it up at arms' length in front of the unseen camera. A second sportsman (see how easily a word with a good pedigree can be bastardised!) then aimed a mighty blow with a spade at the dangling creature's head. The badger skull must have broken into splinters, thousands of them. Then the dogs were given their reward. They were thrown the dead badger.

The image which haunts is when the producer re-ran that sequence. That second time, knowing the viewer had already witnessed the full extent of the atrocity which followed, the action froze as the spade was swung forward.

The explosion of the badger brain was a fraction of a second away. You dared to hope then that the execution would be stayed, that what had happened had not happened. By stopping the action and letting the programme end there a fine judgement had been made. It seemed to say that up to this point there was a choice. The badger could either die or be spared. But because you had already seen the programme, that image said, you know that given the choice, the sportsmen chose to bludgeon the badger into oblivion using a well-practised routine. It said, many badgers have gone like this. We have film of this one. Loudest of all, that one haunting image demanded to know what we are going to do about the sportsmen in our midst.

Clandestine filming of conversations hinted at the motivation of the sportsmen behind such events. They centre on dog breeders. Normally dog breeders breed dogs either because they love dogs, want to make money, or both. Here was a group of men who seemed to be motivated by neither of these things. Rather the objective was to produce a dog of supreme courage to gloat over, its courage tested by the ultimate foe, the ultimate fighter in nature, the hated badger. The hatred stemmed from the fact that sometimes a dog was maimed or failed to measure up to the unequal struggle, an unacceptable weakness in the perverted world of that particular breed of breeder.

It was an ugly film. How could it be otherwise? But among those with whom I discussed it, there was as much revulsion at the technique of the filmmakers as at the sportsmen.

The debate is old enough, and supporters and objectors have polarised long since and it is difficult to be constructive on the subject. The law has done that, and the law says don't do it, and the law banning badger hunts is no easier to enforce than the gassing one, or the poisoning one, and for sure far fewer badgers die from 'sport' than from road accidents. But death on the road is an accident; the sport is premeditated and calls for expertise. In other words, you have to work at it. You have to want to pursue your badger pretty badly. I have no shred of sympathy for badger-digging, and it fails to fall into any definition of sport known to me.

I would have been inclined to leave it at that had not an offshoot of the grapevine coughed up a copy of a book on the subject, written by a terrier worker. My contempt for what I read in this odious little book is such that its title and its author had better remain anonymous. He rages against the laws which have outlawed his sport and cites everything from Handel's Messiah to Nazi Germany in his defence. His assault on the worst excesses of the media (and as a journalist from the age of sixteen no-one knows better than I how excessive that can be) is couched in a degree of hysteria which out-gutters the gutter-press. What is really most offensive is that he planted his soapbox on the moral high ground. He is (ye gods!) a *conservationist* whose sport, far from threatening badgers, actually assists their welfare! A hollow ring of familiarity about that, a well-worn foxhunter's cliché. As for terrier workers who trap a badger and sell it to badger-baiting syndicates to be mutilated by pit-bull terriers, he would have you believe such things simply do not exist, a figment of the gutter's imagination. Well, there is a keeper not far from here who could give him chapter and verse, and dot and comma.

All this in a book which professes to restore a sense of balance to the 'hysterical atmosphere which surrounds the badger'.

Presumably he refers to the 'hysteria' induced by such as David Stephen, who once wrote: 'The man who deliberately sends a terrier to ground to face a badger should resign from the human race.'

To which, as Handel would say, Amen.

14

The End of a Year

M ID-SEPTEMBER, late afternoon. I am sitting on my jacket in the
field edge of the loan, three-quarters of the way over the hill
between the cottage and the Holly Glen. The fields are in stubble. A
kestrel and a sparrowhawk have been working them in the characteristic ways of their tribes – the kestrel is sitting on the wind, the sparrowhawk is punching holes in it.

The tide is high, the mudflats awash, so the curlews have fallen on the
field in huge flocks, a fawn rain. Each time the sparrowhawk crosses
they fly up, circle, land and settle again.

It is warm enough to sit shirt-sleeved and write. The hawthorn and
holly and elder and beech and oak of the loan take care of the wind for
me. Occasionally the wind blows loose a leaf or a twig which falls at
my feet or in my lap, once on to my writing pad as I write the word
'wind'. It is preceded on to the page by the fall of its own shadow.

The warmth goes out of the sun earlier these days. I have been looking
back from the field towards the mountains, but now a mist with an
autumnal edge to it has taken out the mountains. Soon it will blur the
sun and close in on the fields and the Holly Glen. It seems to be trying
to cover the tracks of my year, for it is the end of that year I gave myself to come closer to badgers. Now the badger trail is in place, and
the thread of it is tough and durable. Here and there it is bejewelled
with memories and magic for all its darkness.

I have come to the field edge to write down in some sort of order
the events of the past forty-eight hours, an extraordinary postscript
to my badger year.

Two evenings ago, the moon almost full and risen hugely into an
eastern sky as unclouded and colourless as glass, I walked down to the

Holly Glen. The sunset was in the north-west. Sun and moon stalled briefly in perfect equipoise low over their skylines. I trod a path between orbs, mesmerised by the two lights, the two skies. I might have been a juggler with outstretched arms the width of the landscape, the sun for my left hand, the moon for my right. But I let the sun slip through my fingers and tossed the moon too high and the moment was done.

For half a magical hour, the two skies vied for control of my shadow, the rosehip sky of the north-west, the brightening lemon sky of the east. Finally my shadow leaned tauntingly towards the fading fire. Every tree began to lean away from me, for I walked on the moon's side of the loan, and my shadow climbed trees. I sat down at the crossing place above the Holly Glen to take advantage of a rare northerly breeze in my face, pushing myself as deep into tree shadow as the ballooning moon would allow.

I have heard it said that badgers will not emerge into a full moon and certainly that night's moon in particular and the fawn spaces of the newly-cut stubble fields combined to outshine many a dull span of daylight I could recall. It almost didn't matter: it was electrifying, thrilling, just to be out in it, sharing it with those nocturnal creatures who are emboldened by it. The owls were certainly among them. I never heard such an interminable debate among owls, and in the cool stillness the sounds of their voices traversed miles. In my own trees, above me on the loan and below me in the Holly Glen and along the field edge to the western wood, they wailed and yelped and screeched and screamed and muttered and moaned almost without pause. Surely they too were relishing the perfect night.

I had become a shade more fluent in the language of the night through my first badger year, learning to place footfall in direction and distance by trial and error, and learning (a little less surely) to distinguish one footfall from another. The one which gave me least trouble was the imminent arrival of the badger, for certainly in this neck of the woods he is its heaviest-footed inmate, careless almost, doubtless because his natural environment holds no terrors for him. I now heard him, moonlight or not, approaching surprisingly from the west and along a line I could not place. This turnabout puzzled me: the distance and direction was what I was good at (or at least better at), the diagnosis was the tricky part, but now I was certain only that a badger was coming my way. I shut my eyes the better to listen and close out the visual distractions of the night. The badger was not in the open field, for that was as lit up as an urban highway, but the sound was too distinct to be coming from the other side of the tree-thickened hedge. Somewhere between then ... the ditch! The stubble field's lowest edge tumbled down a shallow bank to a ditch, the bottom of which was perhaps four feet below the level of the field. The hawthorn hedge ran along the far side of the ditch, stopped at the crossing place, then resumed at the higher level of the east field. The badger was in the ditch, thwarting the moonlight.

The sound stopped. A white face thrust forward on a straining neck where the ditch petered out. Then instead of climbing out of the ditch to the corner of the field and over the crossing place by squirming under the fence, he turned left through the hedge and out of sight, and moments later I heard the fence twang on the shadowed side of the Holly Glen. I felt cheated, of course, because if he had crossed where I had expected he would have walked into my camera viewfinder and no badger would ever have been better lit.

Instead, he had taught me something, for when I looked along the ditch and down the side of the Holly Glen I saw at once that he had travelled unhesitatingly down the two blackest corridors of moon-shadow, narrow seams of darkness on a darkless night. He displayed not only acute sense of awareness at the prevailing conditions but also an intimate grasp of his landscape. When I crept down the side of the glen in his wake and then stopped, deeply shadowed myself, to listen, it was to hear only the low-tide sea-and-seabird sounds and the owls contraltoing at the moon. There was no badger sound.

Had he gone to ground inside the Holly Glen? In which case was he returning to it or visiting it from somewhere else, perhaps riding out the brightest moonlit hour below ground? Or had he slipped clean through it? Was he already padding in the short shadow of the hedge which edges the next field?

I had blown my own cover now, so there seemed little point in hanging around. After a brief and fruitless examination of the hedge I stepped back into the moonlit fields and set out for home, only to see a dark, curved shape moving cautiously along the edge of the loan a hundred yards ahead. Another badger?

I put the glasses on the shape, but they were infuriatingly inconclusive. The creature had stopped and was bent over something, probably eating, but its back was to me and it was giving away nothing. I, on the other hand, was giving away everything. I stood in the open field lit up like Blackpool, and the breeze was blowing my scent straight towards it. I crouched and froze so that whenever whatever it was caught my scent I would not appear to be what my scent said I was. I fooled nothing.

My scent duly travelled uphill ahead of me and my 'second badger' turned and metamorphosed into a running fox. What intrigued me then was that, instead of seeking out the shadows as a badger would have done, the fox first ran out into the open field, then stopped, then trotted on, then stopped again, then quietly padded away across the widest stubble field in the county, unsheltered, unshaded, uncaring.

So within the space of five minutes I had learned a little more about fox and badger and how they work, a little more about what it takes to make your way through the hard-white and unforgiving dominion of the moon. I walked home in the shadows, serenaded by owls, and decided to be back at the Holly Glen before dawn.

I dozed until the call of a tawny owl through an open window jerked me awake at 3.30 a.m. The kee-wicks and hoots were punctuated by a woodpeckerish tapping sound. I tiptoed to the kitchen window in the dark in time to see an owl on the bird table, scrabbling among the nuts and ripping lumps from an apple core, and bashing his beak on the wood to clean it. Its timely alarm call was the only time an owl has ever sat on my bird table. I made a flask of coffee, dressed to stave off the dawn chill and was back at the Holly Glen by 4.30 a.m. No syllable of birdlife sounded, nor that of any other living creature. The north sky began to pale, and where it paled the firth caught a band of the same pastel shade and laid it across the water towards me. The tide lay slack and full, the hour windless. I sat by a gate and listened, for the Holly Glen lay in its own unroused web of shadows.

I grew absorbed in the sound of a boat on the water. There is no more fickle conveyor of sound than open water, and I puzzled for a few minutes about just how far away the boat was. I had decided it was perhaps a mile upstream when it hove boldly into view passing beyond the shore-facing end of the glen. I could hardly have been more wrong.

Twice more in the next half hour I was fooled again by boat and ship sounds. Each time they were much closer and visible much sooner than I had placed them.

I decided to shift my position to a gap in the hawthorn hedge where a homing badger might reveal itself out in the open, bold in the quiet and the half-light. Again I heard the drone of a sound far out on the water, but this time, as I struggled to place its source I caught a new note of menace. The sound seemed to come in waves, now distant, now close, now almost under my feet. I looked down and found the source. It *was* under my feet.

Hundreds of wasps thronged the hedge gap a few inches from the ground, or at least from where the ground had been. Now it looked as if a small mine shaft had been let into the hedge bottom, and for yards around the debris of devastation lay in every downhill direction. Fragments of the wasps' papery nest material were everywhere among the heaps of earth and the gouged bank grasses.

Only one creature reduces a wasps' nest to such uselessness – a badger. This had been the night's work, sometime between my leaving the Holly Glen at 11 p.m. and returning at 4.30 a.m. Perhaps if I had stayed out an hour longer I would have seen the culprit slip out below the fence under the holly where a snag of badger hair is a commonplace hallmark. From there to the nest is a short and shadowed pad alongside the hawthorn hedge. I would have seen him home in on the sound far more confidently than I did, growing excited as he neared it, and as the wasps rose to his face, he would attack with uncontrollable frenzy. He would gouge into the bank and slaughter and wreck all that he found there. It is also just possible that given the number of wasps which still survived to throng the ruins, I had disturbed the badger at work.

For the moment, however, I had a more pressing concern. Now that I knew the sound for what it was, my one ambition was to put distance between me and the wasp survivors. I was already too slow. I felt the first sting on my leg through thick cord trousers, and I ran. I made the hundred yards back to the Holly Glen in record time for an athlete in wellies.

As I crossed the fields to the cottage, I wondered how the Holly Glen might be made more amenable to badgers so that they would move in on a more permanent basis. There were many difficulties, not least my own qualms about tampering with nature (although in such an agricultural landscape, what is natural?) and getting the necessary approval of the farmers. I also knew that the root of the idea was that it would make life a lot easier for me, rather than for the badgers. They did, after all, use the place as much as they needed, yet with only a little cosmetic work and feeding encouragement ... The conflict took me over the hill, and subsided only as the pain from the stings began to assert itself, and I started to think instead why it is a badger should so relish the masochistic pleasure of a meal of wasps.

I read Ernest Neal on the subject over breakfast and found little enlightenment. He quotes one report of 300 wasps in a single badger stomach and concludes:

> With these numbers it would seem almost inevitable that some stings would be received, although the quick chopping action of the teeth would kill the majority. I know of no evidence that badgers are immune to wasp venom.

Certainly the badger protects itself by going in with hairs erect so that the wasps cannot reach the skin, but the end of his nose is unprotectable and presumably so are his innards. He must like the taste of his meal with a fervour bordering on addiction, for he seems not to pass up an opportunity of a bellyful of wasps. I rubbed my leg ruefully and spooned honey on to the toast.

The Holly Glen remains an enigma. By late September it was quiet again, its holes filling silently with autumn leaves, although the crossing place badger track stayed wide and flat and occasionally a hair snagged on the fence wire. I saw at first hand just how difficult it would be to tailor the surroundings to suit badgers better. A small herd of cows was let into the adjacent field for a few days and took to drinking and wading in the small burn which flows down one side of the glen. In their coming and going and standing about, they collapsed a section of the burn's bank, and with it that single outside entrance hole. I had not seen it used often, but if the badgers had half a mind to come prospecting here, it was the kind of incident which would incline the other half of their mind to look elsewhere. Perhaps if I had spent my year at the Holly Glen to the exclusion of all else instead of lingering up on the Highland Edge I would have resolved its riddles by now. But I sought the badger in his widest realm and I think I know him better as a result.

The winter lies before me now and, knowing what I now know, I will keep as close an eye on the place as I can and a more thoughtful one. I will read the snows and the clues better, and when spring seeps into the Firth again, and if a sow comes prospecting for a new nursery, I will have done what I can to tempt her to stay. It will not be much, but it might be enough to make a difference.

September wanes. I enter the black wood by the broken sink. Autumn has hold of the place.

Little has changed. It has been a year and a month. The sink still sits like a turnstile. It has grown green, sunk a little lower, and it has broken again. The hidden tension of the wood is less hidden, less tense. Autumn has stained away some of its darkness. The middle-aged sycamore where I sat so comfortless in the beginning has pooled its own roots in gold, autumn's gift. The robin's song is soft and flutey and fluent. His plastic bath is as it was, an inch of water in it.

The earthworks of the badgers have grown vaster. There are several new holes. The magpies, blackbirds and wrens have a tawny owl in their sights. The clamour is hideous.

The wood is no more comfortable to sit in than it ever was, but it was where the year began and where I wanted it to end, a small homage to the conspiracy, for I owed it a substantial debt.

I could now conduct someone as green as I was a year ago round half a dozen setts, one of them halfway up a mountain where eagle shadows fall, one in this black wood where the only shadow which falls is the shape of one leaf printed on another. I could dine out on the stories of the badger and the hare, the badger in the mist with the lapwings, the badger cub and the flash, the badger cub and the owl, the badger that was a mouse, the badger which shunned the moon.

I cannot say that badger-watching at the sett ever hooked me. From the very first, sitting by a hole with a camera felt too much like an ambush to be comfortable. Mostly I have used setts to plot where the badger travels so that I might encounter him on the hoof, the freewheeler, the individualist. If badgers ever do move into the Holly

Glen, it will be my chief delight to find one on the shore, in the fields, grunting along the ditch, testing the memory of the hedge for a new wasp nest. I still have to learn how he climbs the mountain, but because he was on the mountain and because I found him there, I know how the fox climbs the mountain.

I have been content to follow Ratty's advice, to take Badger *as* I find him and *when* I find him because I was not content with the ambush.

I have put some scratched chalk marks of learning on the clean slate with which I began. And like the badger scratchings on the tree bark, they are as durable as they are indelible, even if the tree should fall.

It has been an hour. I leave the wood by the broken sink.

Epilogue

THE WILD BADGER is perilously poised. Note – the *wild* badger. In some parts of Britain his domain has become so urbanised he is no more wild than your garden robin or a farmyard rooster. He has not chosen this state of affairs.

His sett which was once wholly rural has become urban, or suburban. He does not like to move house, however, and his capacity for tolerating disturbance is legendary. So, alas, is our capacity for devouring land. We are forever demanding new housing, new supermarkets, new golf courses, new green field shopping centres, and, worst of all, new roads. The badger which falls prey to these developments is either killed or evicted by them. Or he lives ensnared within them, his wildness diminished.

The fox is better at all this. He has become a successful town dweller, but the badger is fussier. The fox has moved into town and begun to evolve something of a sub-species there, albeit a degraded sub-species. But it is the town which has moved out to the badger. He will neither abandon his traditional territories, nor an instinctive urban reluctance.

It is not good for the badger to be a town dweller. Mostly the human town dwellers who acquire him as a neighbour are delighted by his apparently confiding proximity, but he was never a willing confidant of man. It is just that he has had his choice of location restricted and he prefers to stay put than flit. If he finds a hand that feeds him, and an eye that watches over him in a town, that simply mitigates the sorrow of his urban exile. The fact that we have urbanised badgers is not something of which we should be proud.

A hideous paradox has evolved. The urbanised badger is probably safer than any other badger elsewhere. He has more champions and guardians in town than anywhere else. But he is a badger in a pocket and the crucial social contact with other badger groups and other landscapes is broken. Expanding setts or colonising opportunities for new generations are no longer options. In such circumstances, wildness withers and dies, and he is less badger.

The badger's most concentrated populations are lowland and woodland, which is a pity. Lowland is where we concentrate our own populations, and woodlands we uproot, flatten or fell for our new houses and roads, or use them to pursue our loud leisure. The badger in most lowland woodland is only halfway wild at best, too familiar with too many of us for his own good, or the good of his wildness.

Ernest Neal has tabulated percentages of setts in various habitats across Britain. 'Deciduous and mixed woods, copses' acount for 52.5 per cent of all setts. The next highest percentage, 'Hedge', is 11.4 per cent, and no other habitat makes double figures. Few features of our rural lowland landscape have been more ruthlessly exterminated by modern agricultural practice than deciduous woods and hedges.

Recent badger surveys in central Scotland (where there are many small woods and many badgers, but also half the human population of the country) showed a depressing incidence of sett interference. In one small pocket of urban fringe setts which the grapevine highlighted, more than half had been tampered with, which means dug out by 'the terrier boys', or just vandalised for the same reason that some people kill swans, which is no reason at all.

On the safety in numbers principle, lowland woodland may still offer badger survival the best bet, but what about the quality of survival? As things stand, it offers a fearful prospect for their wildness. And as a reservoir of badgers which drip-feeds upland and Highland territories, it is crucial that it does not feed a diluted wildness into truly wild badger populations.

So how might the wildness of badgers be safeguarded? We start by putting a higher price on our woods and hedges. A change in planning policy to prevent the removal of small woods because they are small would help. Can two small woods be linked by a specifically planted third wood? If so, who cares, who implements and who pays?

Who resists the big developers when local authorities are so impressed and seduced by the size of their cheque-books and the promise of jobs?

Some cloak their intentions in green smoke-screens. A developer employs a badger survey team to demonstrate its environmental awareness, but the survey team complains there was never quite enough time, never quite enough money to do the job thoroughly. Such a survey was drawn to my attention – the grapevine again.

The threat to a significant otter population did not halt the Skye Bridge. Perhaps one day badgers will cross the bridge and colonise badger-less Skye, and the developers will take the credit.

A change in agricultural policy to prevent the removal of hedges would help. Instead of set-aside, why not replant thousands of miles of lost hedges? Smaller fields would be agriculturally less efficient but much more badger-efficient. Some small fields could even become woods. But again, who cares, who implements and who pays?

Is it too much to hope that governments which enact legislation should then be obliged to pay the price of the enactment? A few prosecutions of badger-baiters will not save the wildness of badgers. Real protection of any protected creature means protection of their habitat. In the case of badgers, we need protected woods, and the law should do that too if it is serious about badger protection.

I look longingly at my Highland Edge. For so long its traditional badger territories were empty. Even now it is a frail toe-hold they have on the place. At the beginning of one more new spring in the osprey wood after my badger year I found no trace of badgers, none at all. But I did find a dead heron. It had been shot. It seems the regime which had relaxed long enough to encourage badgers back had toughened again. It may have been coincidence of course, an isolated intrusion by a 'sportsman'. But for as long as the badger presence is on such a knife-edge, isolated incidents can wreak havoc.

The Highland Edge is well wooded. It could be better wooded by far by changing the emphasis from conifer to deciduous or by insisting on a far higher percentage of deciduous trees in new conifer plantations. The law could do that.

Woods alone, however, will not resuscitate badger populations where for too long there have been none. The badger potential of the Highland Edge is considerable. But it needs to be assisted by the introduction and the safeguarding of badger populations until they are well established. A thriving Highland Edge population would be a better reservoir for wild Highland badgers than a lowland one.

Wildness is at ease on the Highland Edge. It is true that there are still keepers who would just as soon shoot a badger as look at it, more impressed by what a badger is capable of than what it actually does. There are, happily, also estates where attitudes to wildlife have shed Victorian prejudice and where introduced badgers would be welcomed.

Then there is the Highland heartland itself, where the badger is a mountaineer among red deer and eagles, and something of a rarity. It is the most treeless place in the land, but it didn't used to be and it needn't be. There is much talk and the beginning of action to initiate the thoughtful reforesting of Highland Scotland. The badger would be one of an enormous range of beneficiaries, and nowhere would the true wildness of badgers be safer.

Most of these possibilities are long term. The re-stocking of the Highland Edge is an immediate possibility. There is woodland enough now to lift endangered lowland badger populations across the central belt and into the Highland Edge, where many more animals could thrive in wildness and ultimately feed into the Highland heartland.

I gave myself a year to watch badgers. I now know that it will not stop just because that year has come and gone. My writer's antennae twitch at every hint of badger on the ground, at every mention of his name. I sense they have a place, like my own, rooted on the Highland Edge, and with luck and nature's co-operation, I expect we will see a lot more of each other. And I hope the conspiracy is listening.